v v v

# Circular Whispers

v v v

A poetry anthology
edited by Kevin Watt

v v v

SOCIAL DESIGN PUBLISHING

Copyright 2016

Social Design, Inc.

http://socialdesignhq.com

San Jose, CA

This book is a work of fiction. Names, characters, places, and incidents either are products of the author's imagination or are used fictitiously. Any resemblance to actual events or locals or persons, living or dead, is entirely coincidental.

Copyright 2017 by Social Design, Inc.

Poetry is copyright the poets listed.

All rights reserved, including the right of reproduction in whole or in part in any form.

For information about bulk purchases, please contact

Social Design, sales@socialdesignhq.com.

# Table of Contents

| | |
|---|---|
| Sarah Zeller - the postcard you didn't buy | 1 |
| Lara Shiner - Drinking Contest | 3 |
| Marta Green - Before The Storm | 4 |
| Cynthia Richards - Little Boy | 5 |
| Rebecca F. Friend - The Dancer | 6 |
| Jacob Lane Archibald - The Night Blossom | 8 |
| Brian F Kirkham - The fish of Paphos Bay | 9 |
| Nancy Lee Armstrong - Old Red Barn | 11 |
| Kevin Meechan - undertones and overtures | 12 |
| Patricia Fritsche - In the Still | 13 |
| James C. Allen - Flames Of Gold | 15 |
| Rj Kram - in her vineyard | 16 |
| David Michael Williams - Winterbach | 18 |
| Phoenix Aradia - What Color Are These Eyes? | 20 |
| Jalia Maley Brodie - and then her mouth caught fire | 22 |
| Kyle Schlicher - Transvestites And Vampiric Leanings | 24 |
| Colleen D. - Cobbled Bridge | 26 |
| Jenny Linsel - My Grandmother's Hands | 28 |
| Gobby Caggiano - The Wreckage on 856 South Rolling Road | 30 |
| Ann Gilchrist - Brutally old | 32 |
| Lacie Simonds - After | 34 |
| Eric Svenson - Before the stirrups came | 36 |
| Emile Calvet - Love unrequited | 37 |
| Matthew Bennett - Dark Seuss suit and tie | 38 |
| Bomo Albert-Oguara - Behind a serrated outline on a November day | 40 |
| Denise a White - Winter Came Today | 42 |
| Nolan Dean Le - A somnambulist's delight | 43 |

| | |
|---|---|
| James Anthony - Presence | 45 |
| Madhu Singh - A street's ablutions | 46 |
| Mark S Green - If a painting could only talk | 48 |
| Caleb Epps - Hybrid Hearse | 50 |
| An Iconoclast Has No Name. - An Affinal Reception | 52 |
| Pamela Charity - Kissed by a Yellow Rose | 53 |
| Paul Goetzinger - First Snow | 54 |
| Rusty Halverson - 4:30 am PST The Beverly Hills Hilton Hotel 2017 Golden Globe Awards | 56 |
| Carlos Guice - The Blue Labyrinth | 58 |
| Autumn Shirley - serenity | 60 |
| George Carle - A Voice In the Orchard | 62 |
| Maggie Z Brown - Anxious Spring | 64 |
| Keith Johnson - Fetching Fats From Urupunga Station to Katherine Meatworks | 66 |
| Steven Gress - Fall's Victim | 68 |
| Joseph John Taras Kushnir - Gathered In a Piney Circle | 69 |
| Jon Richards - View from Carn Brea | 70 |
| David I Mayerhoff - Cold Contrasts | 72 |
| Danielle Linggar - The Sun Rises in the East | 74 |
| Lawrence Mosieri - Disney Springs Is Come Of Age | 76 |
| Lisa O' Mahony - The Man in the Attic | 78 |
| Samantha Cheshire - Fleeting Affections | 80 |
| Maxwell E. Hoover - swimming | 82 |
| Celeste Jackson - Take Your Pamphlets Somewhere Else | 84 |
| Chelsea Rainford - Finnimbrun | 89 |
| Aditya Rao - The Sun | 90 |
| Rachael S. Mcdermott - footslog | 91 |
| Alona Perlin - The Joy of Winter | 93 |
| Winter Kage - Silent | 94 |

| | |
|---|---|
| Alwyn Barddylbach - Enchanted | 96 |
| Kaylie Rosenberry - Shadow On the Snow | 97 |
| Simona Prilogan - Seeking my own | 99 |
| Trudi Ruth Benford - Thirst | 100 |
| Tracy Banks - Fire | 101 |
| Kevin Mathew Panackal - Mind Street | 102 |
| Dylan Church - Ballroom of Blisters | 104 |
| Lesly Frances Finn - The Ball Gown | 107 |
| Sarah Gosa - Grand Isle | 108 |
| Gc Basher - Finely Crafted Ending | 109 |
| Bianca Szasz - Jokes | 111 |
| Finbarr Harkin - Poseidon's Beasts | 112 |
| Sujata Baruah - My Sweet Valentine | 114 |
| Estella Sanders - Ohio State University | 116 |
| Drew Lagoon - Bone Breathing | 117 |
| Kyle Schlicher - Quaaludes And Nyquil | 119 |
| Patricia A Edwards - Just Beyond my Touch | 123 |
| Stephen Jackson - Inheritance | 124 |
| Nicholas 'Georgie' Scott - Somewhere In The Attic | 126 |
| Bharati Nayak - A Tree I Am | 127 |
| Paul Hernandez - Silent Light | 129 |
| Terence M Sheppard - Amongst the cold and the grey | 131 |
| Gregory Francis Schrupp - Empty air of butterfly sunshine II | 135 |
| Catherine Welch - Untitled first post | 137 |
| Andy Sprouse - Silence and Solemnity of Snow | 138 |
| Tina King - I want to be the sunbeam | 140 |
| George Robinson - At The Beach | 142 |
| Ludvig Hoel - Onward bound we go | 143 |
| Mary Beth Holland - Taste the Amber | 144 |
| Ritika Singh - I Pray | 145 |
| Allison W - The Lady in Blue | 146 |

| | |
|---|---|
| Astrid Tejero - One Love, Two Souls Equally Yoked | 148 |
| Jacob Mashburn - Fall | 151 |
| Vernoica Thibodeaux - Sisters of the Blood Chalice | 152 |
| Tanya Kanakaole - Snug Harbor | 153 |
| Mark Andrew James Terry - Too Frost To Know | 154 |
| Stefan Roudan - naked clown | 156 |
| Annabelle Molyneux - And She Danced | 158 |
| David Michael Williams - The Whispers of The Night | 162 |
| Stuart W. Bowen, Jr. - Oh, Jesus! | 163 |
| Mary C Galindo - Nature's Miracle | 164 |
| Christine Pingry - Winter's Break | 165 |
| Kali Krontz - Eager | 166 |
| Claudia Sprague - comfort food | 168 |
| D P Morgan - I fell again today. | 169 |
| Susanne Donoghue - Why? | 170 |
| Ketriana Yvonne - Water is Life | 172 |
| Holly Parker - Live in the moment | 174 |
| Nancy Mendi - Southern Charm | 175 |
| Tristan P. Scarbrough - Yuki-Onna | 176 |
| Anamarija Celinić - I still do | 178 |
| Deb Brat - Thoughts can be blank | 180 |
| Charlie Rankin - A Cosmos of Darkness and Light | 181 |
| Emma Wilson - Him | 183 |
| Paul Miller - My first poem as an adult. | 184 |
| Dakota Grinslade - Hatchet | 186 |
| Nicholas Scott 'georgie' - Silence Falls | 187 |
| Mikhail Dmitrievich Bashkirov - The Better | 188 |
| Stephen Hollins - Turquoise Light of Aitutaki | 190 |
| Patricia A Edwards - Beyond the Desert | 193 |
| Raymond Butt - anemophilous Currents.. | 195 |
| Jaira Zeck - (like a rose) | 199 |

| | |
|---|---|
| Niky Smith - No Light Without Darkness | 202 |
| Carolyn J Bayne - Peace Maker | 203 |
| Kathleen Hannah Marshall - love is like a passionate night out | 204 |
| Geoffrey Barnes - Her | 205 |
| Bosadiq Hashim - The Spark | 207 |
| Michael Orem - Tear The Leash | 209 |
| Vernoica Thibodeaux - A Tribute to Aphrodite | 211 |
| Joanne Zylstra - What I See | 212 |
| Joanne Zylstra - This Night | 214 |
| David H Hussey, Jr - We're Not The Ones | 215 |
| Kiki Weber-Suarez - Words | 217 |
| Peter Boadry - Dear Mom (Today's your Birthday) | 218 |
| Debra Digioia - A Moment Away | 219 |
| Brenda Joyce Mixon - God Is Looking At You | 221 |
| Roma Zerangue - "Mom" | 223 |
| Pasquale F. Lorina - Go Away | 224 |
| Dakota Grinslade - Mayhem & Chaos | 225 |
| Joseph Benjamin Hobbs - € \|-\| o o $ 3 /\/ | 227 |
| Annie Foster - The Wilting Flower | 229 |
| Ashley Cantrelle - Your Love of Life or Life of Love? The Latter. | 231 |
| Diana Viguri - You Know My Name.. Grief | 235 |
| Kayla Brothers - Dreams | 238 |
| Rebecca Lyle - Night | 239 |
| Antonio Rivera Iii - Yauco | 241 |
| Jason Robert Van Pelt - Heart Omnibus! | 245 |
| Joanne Zylstra - The Visit | 247 |
| Stefan Roudan - Lets run | 249 |
| Vernoica Thibodeaux - The Tears of my Ancestors | 251 |
| Geovanny Medina Arteaga - A Forever Impure Life | 253 |
| Arthur C. Liggins - Just Like You | 255 |

| | |
|---|---|
| Ronald Watson-Bolden - Black Like Me | 257 |
| Stephen Kelly - My Stand for Love | 258 |
| Robert Moody - They don't want you loving me | 261 |

[ Sarah Zeller ]

# the postcard you didn't buy

Bathed
in the fiber of Spring
days tumbled
within wild parables

reflections of mountains
painted with fire
sparking hellos
to dark sunshine
upon warm-tipped lips

wet within mist rolling like silk
cradled in the dance of sky and cloud
milk-blue in it's cooling

watch them shape-shifting...
secretly
where the wind whispers
across the swaying tree tops

a clockwise dust
settles
on the lithe scent
of ripening wildflowers

that ribbon the sound

in creamy amber

deepening to vibrant plum

_____

Sarah Zeller resides with her husband and two children from Lakeport Michigan. She is a published author, a poet and a dreamer. Allpoetry.com/Blindspot

[ Lara Shiner ]
# Drinking Contest

Paw prints of a leopard
squelched thick on her tongue,
and her lungs are smoky peaks,
liver an old bear grown silver--

From her hand she spills
the spirit-sea wild past her teeth
wherein cliff stones catch
shore's fist upon their face

(but don't spit) and down
the potion tumbles to her core,
forest fed on the bottle's milk she rains--
and as the tavern's shouts eclipse her ears,

she's earned her nature's praise.

---

Lara lives in Louisville, Kentucky. She draws inspiration from art, nature, and her piano. She's currently working on a collection of poems for stand-alone publication. Allpoetry.com/Soundfable

[ Marta Green ]

# Before The Storm

It is freezing tonight and the cows are sitting,
on the frost covered grass like living piles of fur.

Bovine covered in winter coats,
like from the wool of freshly shorn sheep.

Walking to the barn so I can put out a bale of hay,
it is as cold as the moments before a snow storm.

Holding my hands over my icy ears,
I hear the howling wind in the barn rafters.

Coming into the barn, I walk through the doors,
smiling gratefully.

_____

I am a writer of poetry. It has been interesting learning more about poetry and I have had a lot of fun doing so. This poem is dedicated to my number fan, my father, Norman Diaz. Allpoetry.com/Marta_Green

[ Cynthia Richards ]
# Little Boy

Oh Little Boy

I never knew

But always touch your hand

Within

The sadness cried

To suddenly

Subside

A low

A wake

That wonders

Why

In all the wandering stars

---

Cynthia Richards is from Los Angeles. Symbolist in art and writing. Humanist. Allpoetry.com/CynthiaRichards

[ Rebecca F. Friend ]

# The Dancer

Sand saturated
by waves
is firm beneath
her bare feet,
like the stage of
polished hardwood
in the abandoned theater
of her adolescence.

A beach towel
hugs slender hips,
purple lotus blossoms
and pink flamingos
flipping in the breeze,

make-shift substitute
for a ballet skirt
of white tulle and
silver gauze.

Using a distant sailboat
as her spot,
the dancer performs
one fouetté turn

in a whirlwind of platinum hair
before her stamina stalls.

She recalls an encore
performance
of ten dizzying spins,
singing violins and
a standing ovation;

facing the ocean, she curtsies
and bathes in the surf's applause.

———————

Mother, author and retired social worker. I am a native of Charlotte, North Carolina, finding my voice in poetry. Allpoetry.com/Becki_Friend

[ Jacob Lane Archibald ]

# The Night Blossom

In the mist of the standing stones
Towering on the hills of Moy Tara
The rose of Danu blooms in the night
Its crusted white petals, spread
In the might of the full moon on Samhain eve
Its gleam shines on its glossy leaves
As the rose, crescent white stands tall
As the wind hits the towering stones
Blowing the voices from the sea
Wind struck, and wood hardened
The night blossom stands tall
      In the mist of the standing stones...

---

I was born in Amarillo, TX. Had the hard knox life of living the streets and drugs. Gang life consumed me than an amazing blessing saved me from that fallen grace. And so i honor him daily... Allpoetry.com/archibald

[ Brian F Kirkham ]
# The fish of Paphos Bay

As the sun rays shine
over the starboard side
of the incoming plane
it casts a shadow.

And shimmering in the shadow,
shiny little silver fish
shimmer in the water
swimming in the blue sea

Travelling 'tween rocky pools
and ancient stones
conversing with
cocky crustaceans

Shifts between the light and dark
A pair of alien feet appear
Aware of oncoming danger
they attack from the rear.

So on mass, they circle and nip
the alien, on his summer trip

In respect of their brothers and sisters regret,

caught up in the fisherman's net.

---

A poet from Salford, England. I Like to write pieces on historical places, buildings and objects. Currently volunteering for imperial war museum north, where I help visitors within the galleries. Allpoetry.com/InkdropK

[ Nancy Lee Armstrong ]

# Old Red Barn

There is an old red barn,
Just below my Grandma's house.
Where the boards are coming loose.
So is the siding and the door.
The wind howls a haunted noise,
Even to the old wooden floor.
For this is where my heart belongs
These are the memories, I long for.
The times of climbing up into the loft,
To jump off into the hay.
Beneath me, Grandma milks the cows,
While feeding the kitty cat,
As she licks her paws away,
Grandma and I gather the buckets,
To carry the milk to the house,
When the cat runs a little mouse.
Into the old red barn,
How I love living on a farm.

---

I write poems that are inspirational to me. Some of my poems I have experienced in my real life. Like this poem, 'The Old Red Barn'. Allpoetry.com/Nanarm45

[ Kevin Meechan ]

## undertones and overtures

wet, as perished thoughts

we fell asleep on the wind,
flouting fancy ideas

dead men's whistles,
drown out that awful silence

afforded silken sheets,
and ornate urns

in the heartbeat of comfortable living

what longs to be held,
is hollow

---

Kevin Meechan is from Scotland and complains regularly about a lack of sleep. He enjoys long walks, often wishing he could master the art of sleepwalking. Allpoetry.com/kevin_meechan

[ Patricia Fritsche ]

# In the Still

It was a day
wrung out from sheer
lack of uncloaked laughter.

Involved on plane with pigeon coos
shoulders scream
is everything clean enough?

Minute wisps of discontent
last cut
swiped against plate's smiling porridge

neighbor
on high alert growing pains
of constant shadows
bullying

spills seem ever growing
stern as sails
hanging out clothes smell of city breath.

Yet, this existence
cowers not

to spit racing towering, from below.

Arriving it babbles
chewing on
discontent from gray film
mocking new sun

to face dusk's eyelids
blind to anything else,
    it begs for a ray of evolving.

---

Composition from then and now is the sowing and harvesting in memories garden; the sharing of those senses, maybe discovering in each day a special outlook. With this my passion continues to grow. Allpoetry.com/Perrier

[ James C. Allen ]

# Flames Of Gold

God how we loved
until our flesh turned
in upon itself like an
alchemist's palette gone
astray.

When he fell I detached
from the sap
surrendered the source
of my once impervious
existence.

One after another
they descend
like kites which once fluttered
out of human sight,
glorious as rainbows
now gone brown.

---

James C. Allen was reared in Clinton, Mississippi. He began writing poetry in fifth grade to the consternation of most around him. He settled into a style which he terms 'Psychological Poetry.' Allpoetry.com/James_C._Allen

[ Rj Kram ]

# in her vineyard

purple plump
grapes under
green leaves are
glazed wet in the
grey rain

white lightning
flashes
on pine lattice
that sags
and creaks
from heavy wind

I fight
to brace it in the
cold thick mud
that puddles
at my feet

and hear her
in the thunder
begging me
to let her go

*****

I reach
for the heavy vine
and pluck
one grape

it tastes sour
like our parting

glimpses of her hair
appear on the sky
with white flashes
as leaves shiver
in the wind
wet like the hem
of her dress

she haunts me
in every cold slap
of the rain

---

I write to relax, to feel alive, and to get on paper what's been thumping in my head. This piece was a collaboration with Elegia. Allpoetry.com/RJ_Kram

[ David Michael Williams ]

# Winterbach

Floating flakes of lace now fall,
Lightly dusting the world white,
Icebobs dangle from roof eaves,
Glisten in the morning light.

Scarlet berries hold their hue,
Amid the mantle of snow.
The cardinal sings winter's tune,
From outside of my window.

I warm my feet by the fire,
And drift away in a book.
Sporting wintertides new wears,
Knitted scarf and mitted look.

My lodgings nested serine,
Warm with a candle lit glow.
As crackerjack houses string,
In an alabaster row.

Barren trees twist toward the sky,
Their fingers without a leaf.
Embedded soft shapes of grey,
Harken the season's motif.

Mike Williams is a poet from Texas. Poetry became my passion to express myself and cope with life's trials. The word well spoken and a deed well done is liberating. Allpoetry.com/Mike_Williams_1

[ Phoenix Aradia ]

# What Color Are These Eyes?

A special twilight,
storm's rolling in;
the air is heavy,
the light is dim.

The fervent sunshine,
only sits in pools.
Overcasting shadows,
the mercury cools.

I see somber slate,
staring back at me.
An ashen spirit,
made of concrete.

Behind flannel glass,
are clouds passing by.
Silver sharks swimming,
elicit a sigh.

Like charcoal newsprint,
or smudged lead cement.
The dappled iron
of a Confederate.

Wrapped in the wisdom
of the oldest age;
or the steel resolve
behind blinding rage.

———————

Phoenix Aradia is an eclectic amateur writer, residing in the United States. She is a resolute animal welfare advocate, and has the greatest respect for all living creatures. Allpoetry.com/Phoenixaradia

[ Jalia Maley Brodie ]

# and then her mouth caught fire

exhaust pours from her face
as she breathes
taste of gas, hot on her tongue
bitter, with a hint of spice—
cajun, if you will

"tonight is the night she'll burn up
into nothing," says God

earlobes, lined with liquid blisters,
bleed pillows of smoke,
reminiscent of vile cirrus clouds

digging teeth into her flesh—
biting, famished

swollen pockets of blood cluster
within rows of red gums

and, protruding loosely from them,
like bats upside down in caves
are well-lit cigarettes,
wearing crowns of hot orange—

instead of the typical

32 teeth

---

Jalia Maley Brodie (born on January 28th, 1999) is from a small town in Tennessee. She was inspired to write at an early age, and admires authors such as Edward Gorey, Stephen King, and Tim Burton. Allpoetry.com/un_chien_andalou

[ Kyle Schlicher ]

# Transvestites And Vampiric Leanings

color the night
black
blue
backing

stranger walking
with
his
hands
in his pockets

lamplights
halo
a circle
in the damp air

cigarette's red flare
fading
with
the
curling smoke

gleaming eyes
follow

the
path
of the light
tracing
shadows
in the stillness

figure in black
wanders
closer
hollowed cheeks
nostrils alert

hello,
how are you doing,
comes
the
opening.

---

I live in Gulfport, Florida. I make a daily attempt to write and I have in my possession the one and only original Bullwinkle Leaf. Allpoetry.com/Slickone

[ Colleen D. ]

# Cobbled Bridge

a fire burns in the forest deep glowing
in flames that rustle leaf-like, amber, red
and Autumn's splendor burnt orange showing

cobbled bridge drums hollow upon my tread
arching o're the bustling stream, while I dream
cool crisp air softly following in my stead

in my hand, Eve's apple, cider moonbeam
both tart and sweet 'neath skies of clearest blue
fragrant ripened crimson orbs dangling gleam

temptation to be plucked, tasty adieu
the Harvest Moon floats like a toy balloon
hovering pumpkins in fields hitherto

lengthening shadows climbing daylight swoon
to reach the twilight 'fore winter descends
and seek there warm shelter where lovers croon

---

I have lived in New England for most of my life, where I find much of my inspiration for writing. About a year ago, I discovered poetry and have begun what I expect

will be a lifetime love affair! Allpoetry.com/
Colleen_2017

[ Jenny Linsel ]

# My Grandmother's Hands

My Grandmother's hands told many tales
Of scrubbing steps and broken nails
Hand-washing clothes in enamel sink
Red football socks turned white towels pink
When not baking cakes at the old gas stove
Rag-rugs with old scraps of material she wove
Pantry shelves filled with powdered egg
Homemade rice pudding sprinkled with nutmeg
Sea-coal burning on an open coal fire
Bread on a toasting fork burning like a pyre
Grandma plumping up pillows from beneath granda's head
Applying ointment to sores caused by being confined to bed
Hours spent at auctions bidding with her hand
Buying an incomplete bed wasn't what she planned
Back home in time for tea, crumpets and homemade strawberry jam,
I can still recall the smell of it, bubbling in the pan
Switching tv channels with a flick of her wrist
That's how we did it back then, when remotes did not exist
Working hard all of her life, meeting everyone's demands

Every line and wrinkle told a story

On my Grandmother's hands

---

I am from Hartlepool in the United Kingdom. I write poetry because I find it very cathartic. My poems are usually about things I remember from my past. Allpoetry.com/Jenruff2001

[ Gobby Caggiano ]

# The Wreckage on 856 South Rolling Road

Bathtub brimming with roses
Tobacco kisses he
Brushes past her
Hand on her aproned waist
Just long enough

Sorry that I kissed you inebriated
O not sorry

Red pigment clotting
She stands holding the bagel knife, sliced
Open waiting
Watching the two bearded men
Marshmallow dreams bars and fancy vodka
The smell of root beer and indecision
wafting
blue eyes versus brown

My place or yours?

It smells like sex in here, not
The cologne and fresh shampoo
kind of scent she'd imagined
Wine on their breath

Your thrifted sweater feels like angel wings.

A worst and favorite sin; falling
In love on a couch on a dorm room bed
On Thanksgiving in a parked car at 5:26am
In the backroom of the coffee shop
Mocha syrup dripping from the countertop

I love you;

careful,
If you say that enough,
you'll start to believe it

---

Gobby Caggiano is from Baltimore, Maryland and graduated high school in 2016. She works at Starbucks and scribbles bits of poetry on napkins during her breaks before spilling coffee all over them. Allpoetry.com/Rosesandwhimsy

[ Ann Gilchrist ]

# Brutally old

undone by her tongue
wretchēd in her eyes
despise castrates the gonads from his glee
a thumbprint grows so heavy
it defoliates a spread
and glints a bald surrender on his head

resentment wriggles wormlike
from the caverns in his ears
peering from his nostrils with a sniff
bulging discontentment
in the waistband of his shorts
and jaundice in his brittle curling nails

he shuffles in her wake
has-been of her speech
no selfie-youth to hide his stale decay
he opens the front door
to a sidewalk in the rain
and writes a further chapter of the same

his spine is stooped in slopes
of social sentence
edentulous the drought of his discourse

whistling an ill-fit from his cake-hole
like winds of bowels so suddenly dispersed

the gutter holds up mirrors to the drizzle
passing traffic breaks it up in sloppy shards
decisively he two steps to the busway
and leaves the coroner his calling card

---

Soulo is originally from Scotland but has called Australia home since 1982. She began writing as a child but has become more absorbed in her poetry in much more recent times. Allpoetry.com/Soulo

[ Lacie Simonds ]

# After

Sheets silhouette lovers' forms;
lounging in soft light.

Voices travel lazily through the air,
caressing exposed skin -
touching the homes of lips
minutes before.

Eyes meet with
mirrored chemistry.
The urge to touch again,
a gentle tug within.

The gaze breaks
as lashes flutter down,
brushing cheeks
still flushed with energy.

Sweat sticks,
once slick.
Reminding both
of what had been.

---

Lacie is originally from Dietrich, Idaho. She is now a member of the Armed Forces and uses poetry as a way to express her thoughts and emotions. Allpoetry.com/Salig

[ Eric Svenson ]

# Before the stirrups came

Sheen of my white skin
Whitecap rests upon the swell and surge
Of a thunderous black wave urge

To cavalcade crush
All foreign footprints
On southern sands once bleached and breached

Only by alchemist wind
And sorceress sun
While concubine moon hung in abeyance

Glowing her luminescent knowledge
Down upon loincloth clad innocents
Python dancing around flickering fires

Before the stirrups came
Rhythmic tribal drum beat
Celebrated unpleated passion

---

Poet, philospher, short story writer living in Paternoster, Western Cape, South Africa. I've published four poetry/short story volumes, most recently Dancing with Dragonflies. Allpoetry.com/eric_svenson

[ Emile Calvet ]

# Love unrequited

Stone faced as a farting bulldog
lantern jaw clamped, placidly returning
the sternest human stare

Inscrutable as a crapping bulldog
calmly laying a fresh load of faeces
onto the trimmest lawn

She'd keep slurping her vanilla milkshake
unflinching eyes driven deep into mine
on the Champs Elysées

Composed, she drank the mead of my sorrow,
unrelenting, her vestal-like candour
stoking up dark desire

Transfixed before her immaculate cheek
I let the burn sink down my screaming flesh
The sun set in Paris

---

A free hopper currently based in Paris. To me Poetry has been the strongest prop whether I read it or try to write it Allpoetry.com/Calvet_Emile

[ Matthew Bennett ]

# Dark Seuss suit and tie

bored and chewing, on a sad memory bone.
gnawing away like its nothing new.
dressed in the clothing, of the criminal.
light gray, the suit and tie.

crisp and clean.
hide and seek, of personality.
smiles of scared charm..
winning over the unexpected.

hand shakes, sign on the dotted line.
daily bread from children's table.
loser, victim are to blame.
cold walks another one born.
the tally counts a good day,
of doing business.

taxes payers room robe paid to sit.
on the wall in fairytales we trust.
dressed in the clothing, of the criminal.
dark blue pin stripes. the suit and tie.

best money can buy.
hump back hump back,

crooked letter of the law.

spewing technicalities.

contract signed bottom line.

client sentence and fined.

cheap bottle of wine,

poured over laughter.

lady Justice, has been dismissed.

---

I'm 49, born and raised in Michigan. I've been a machinist for 20 years. I have eight kids - 5 girls and 3 boys. Married the first girl I dated, but 30 years after the fact. I love to manipulate the meaning of words. Allpoetry.com/Matt_D_Bennett

[ Bomo Albert-Oguara ]

# Behind a serrated outline on a November day

The new autumn freshness
is gone out of the window in
the month of October. November
ushers in the farmer's scourge.

As I stand looking out the window
held prisoner of this house, I wait
for the trees to shed their chaffed
leaves one by one. Today, as every

other day, the sun comes shinning
through, shattering into fragments
of rainbow colors as it lands on the
window. I look beyond it and see

a serrated outline of rooftops jutting
into the horizon; smoke-filled chimneys
oozing white clouds of winter fires. The
sycamore swathes in desolate wintry

purview; night casts its somnolent grip;
I am hungry; the leaves have stopped

falling; grim, mountainous Glasgow lays
far, far away in the winds. The sycamore

is pregnant again; she will yield green leaves
and I will be waiting by the window once more
when dawn wakes us all, to the sound of summer
London.

———————

Bomo Albert-Oguara is from the Southern coast state of Bayelsa, Nigeria. He is a writer who cherishes his art of poetry - a way of speaking in colors on a varying range of topics private, but mostly public . Allpoetry.com/Bomo_Albert-Ogua

[ Denise a White ]

# Winter Came Today

Winter came today
geese flew in formation
a salutation to the storm
brewing in the southwest

A whiteout, blizzard
not because of the light snow
but winds gusted to pick it from the ground
covered birch, oak, pine branches, caused drifts

Windswept with white paint
the landscape a silent vision
went undisturbed in twilight hours
a testimonial to the truth of the north

We came over the horizon and wept.

---

Denise A is currently living in the Midwest, but is looking to move soon to the Oregon coast. She has written a poetry book, Butterflies Will Come and is working on her third book, a poetic memo. Allpoetry.com/Denise_A

[ Nolan Dean Le ]

# A somnambulist's delight

With my naked eyes
His body bathed in the morningtide
Inhabit spaces between the blinds
The rise and falls of his nude figure
Only rays of sun as his armor
Curved lines of an abstract bodyscape
Contemptible as a ghost
discovering the morning light.

A commander to the dream
Nothing can stop his momentum
Except the sun luminously sheathed
While reality ties to the hands of time
Shadows played against the sheets

I wish I had always known
The dewy taste of his skin
As I write poetry with my tongue
And cast blame to the spirits.

A legend of a somnambulist's delight
Conjuring in the behemoth of expectations
In the shades between the morning sun
and the last nuances of fun.

Nolan Dean Le lives in a tree house on a ranch with a singing Pomsky. He writes poetry while everyone else sleeps and dances to his own drumbeat. Allpoetry.com/Nolan_Dean_Le

[ James Anthony ]
# Presence

In the doorway of a cottage
a side-winding wind

charms

the decayed leaves
lifting a skeleton of brown and red

bones

the evening sunlight
coagulates

---

James is from Ireland. He enjoys poetry and attends creative writing classes which he finds enjoyable and educational. Allpoetry.com/James_Anthony

[ Madhu Singh ]

# A street's ablutions

A few hours into dawn
while the street is still asleep
it gets a cursory cleansing
with a long handled stiff broom
at the hands of a grumpy jamadar.

Hurried rough strokes
on the tar smeared cheeks
wake the groggy street
which yawns dust
off its surface
to obscure the trees lining it
from whose branches
crows and mynahs
have long flown
in search of worms
but chicks in nests
twitter their reply.

Barefooted housemaids
with silver anklets
and hennaed soles
step out to sprinkle water

from Aluminum buckets
on the risen dust
which settles down
as a wet film
back on the street.

---

Madhu Singh was born in India and currently resides in New Delhi. She is an MBA with experience in the IT sector. In her free time she enjoys writing freeverse, ghazals and english language haiku. Allpoetry.com/tuni

[ Mark S Green ]

# If a painting could only talk

Embrace the yellow rapeseed
let it brush through your fingers
ramble amongst pastures of intense sunshine
the golden pigment
stain the palms of your hands
nature's nectar luring you in
painting you as one.

Mercury rising
glowing hot
the belly of the sun
passion flares within you
full of joy, intrepid excitement
heart beating as bees scurry in a hurry
meandering within the wisp of the gentle breeze.

The scent of early summer
blends honeysuckle with toffee apple
sweet taste lingers on the tip of your tongue
like chocolate
melting
your mind ignites with sensory overload
childhood memories at the fun fair.

Then a blue jay glides
just above the field
in line with a solitary cloud
to the centre of this yellow ocean
where giant oak tree stands proud,
its rugged bark and vivid green leaves
waving to everyone and everything.

---

Mark Green is an established poet from Stafford, UK. As an author, Mark has seen his poems printed in numerous anthologies & magazines. See his book 'Rhymes from the Book of Life' at Kindle, Kobo etc. Allpoetry.com/Mark_Green

[ Caleb Epps ]

# Hybrid Hearse

A sigh punctures
the fragile fabric
in the facade,
dims the decay
of severed ceilings,
dissolves the barriers
of fireplaces,
paints over the peepholes.

Along the tendril,
after cooling my hands
in the whirlpool,
I crawled into this car,
it's model marked plainly
by bent bumpers,
gibbous gauges
and gnarled navigation interface.

Cramped coffin of my coma,
caretaker cottage of my craziness,

the sedan swivels onto the shoulder,
off shattered streets;
in the hole of the hood

sprout sickly specters

of twigs and torsos.

A supple sapphire

crashes the canvas,

calls on the cloudburst,

and disperses the downfall

of rotting rooftops,

liquefies the limits

of telescopes,

paints over the peepholes.

---

Caleb Epps is an amateur writer of prose and poetry from Omaha, Nebraska. He is flattered and delighted to be a part of this collection. Allpoetry.com/eppypen

[ An Iconoclast Has No Name. ]
# An Affinal Reception

beyond Oregon shores, the dance floor a sighing mirror:
wings flap, beaks dunk, heads swivel, repeat-
reverse order and instigator.

Overture complete, they float towards
invisible marks stretched on ripples.
Nature's starter pistol calibrated by

magnetism ricocheted their earshot. They're off-
wingspans splayed foray of webbed tiptoes
ladling the champagne sync, breasts toasting ceremony

their necks held like arrow-serpent amalgams
graded on the curve of a longbow. Hastening miracle
akin to Jesus, (Peter not quite) stride by stride ten meters

along a wavering altar ruffled nuptials consummate as
avian yawls set sail, paired to a renascent jubilee
bride and groom grebes plume in honeymoonlight.

---

I am originally from Detroit, Michigan but now reside in Las Vegas, Nevada. I've been writing for 17 years now; I love the diversity of forms and the opportunity to express myself. Allpoetry.com/Laughing_Wolf

[ Pamela Charity ]

# Kissed by a Yellow Rose

Dewey yellow rose petals
blow from the garden
and land against my cheeks
imagine being kissed by a yellow rose

A war between
winter and spring
fill the air
opportunity given
through the kiss of a yellow rose

---

Pamela Charity is from Elizabeth City, N.C. She is an uprising poetress and brings forth intriguing and powerful poems to her readers. Allpoetry.com/Prcgemini

[ Paul Goetzinger ]

# First Snow

Long promised storm, covers mountain forests
Spreading south into suburban lowlands
Afghans of white, cloak urban paths
City crews and plow drivers
Hurry to clear municipal streets
While citizens shoveling sidewalks
Remove weighted blankets of white

Businesses losing desired power
Amid blizzard like conditions
Local children, frolic in snow drifts
Putting finishing touches on motionless men
While miniature avalanches
Flow lazily downward from white covered knolls

Teams of volunteers, flexing long dormant muscles
Pushing cars up a hill
Cold air, chilling the heart
Neighbors, walking carefully down icy tracks
Wind chill, dropping as dusk settles
Straining exerted lungs

The coldest days have arrived
Earth, turns its face from the sun

While the shortest day of the year approaches
Remaining leaves of the autumn slip quietly from the trees
As the flow of life slows down and turns inward
La Nina settles in for the season
Leaving white-frosted lawns to sleep until spring

---

Paul Goetzinger is a former college educator, poet and writer from Des Moines, Washington. He uses his poetry and essays to mentor and inspire his friends and former students. Allpoetry.com/Paul_Goetzinger

[ Rusty Halverson ]

# 4:30 am PST The Beverly Hills Hilton Hotel 2017 Golden Globe Awards

The dawn hesitated
Not camera ready
Tails and cummerbunds
Buttons, laces
Await the gate
Black on black
The pause is crisp
A comma
Weighted wings
Perched upon the edge.

Hold the horses
By their halters
Bitten by the
Hidden sun
The plan half-baked
Half awake
Wait again
Its fated.

Stars are winking
Wrinkles are merely
Planned obsolescence


Dawn and motion
Picture perfect
Arrivals to the venue

---

Born in Charleston, SC in 1961, Rusty trained as an actor at the University of North Carolina School of the Arts and studied voice under James Dodding at the City Literary Institute in London, England. Allpoetry.com/Rgrhalverson

[ Carlos Guice ]

# The Blue Labyrinth

his fingers ran like mice
nibbling, on morsels of sonorous, notes
along every nook and cranny,
along the neck of the
age-old, guitar.

his myth transformed his music
when his magical, mythic, movements
trapped old man blues.

a blue minotaur, suspended
in a labyrinth of licks, riffs, and phrases,
lost to meandering; mazy, and
musical passes.

for when
his blue tones take you
to Daedalic places,
no golden thread
can ever bring you back.

---

JuiceVerse is a native of Cleveland, Ohio. He gets his inspiration from reading poets like Paul Laurence Dunbar, Langston Hughes, Gwendolyn Brooks, and Maya Angelou. Allpoetry.com/JuiceVerse

[ Autumn Shirley ]

## serenity

I long for the stars
lighting up the sky
with mountains in the background
and fire flies
oh what a beautiful view
a nice big full moon

the summer days
and heat waves
the smell of fresh cut
grass and clothes
freshly hung
on the line
sun tea
and watermelon

camp fires
roasting marshmallows
family
telling stories

peacefully resting
in the Lord's glory

JESUS has been my inspiration through my entire life, through my trails of life i have learned to become a better soul full of love and inspiration that i can share with the world. Allpoetry.com/faithful_lamb

[ George Carle ]

# A Voice In the Orchard

Sadder now I wander
down by the orchard
where cider apples grow
and the spirit of youth
blossomed with you

I hear a voice
long since gone
rustle the leaves
like the wind
blows through Autumn

brown and curled
stalked words
of childhood return
blown and swirled
the memories mine

fifth from the end
the one I would climb
gaunt and dead now
the silence of peace
no words to be found.

I am a retired family doctor from Scotland still in the UK. I have published in several magazines and won a few poetry prizes. Allpoetry.com/Gcarle7575

[ Maggie Z Brown ]

# Anxious Spring

I have seen
the new season's lines:
white, capering on green,
curls tight like astrakhan,
tails whisking a watery
sunshine.

Yet my joy is constrained
by an anxiety of wire
stretched taut - old winter's
shattering breath is not all spent,
he snarls, shows teeth in
cold snaps

  and

    I don't think I can bear
to make slinky skins
into warm hats
for another still born year.

---

I live in the beautiful Tasman, New Zealand. I write poetry and short stories, and tend towards subjects involving the natural world. Allpoetry.com/Margrit

[ Keith Johnson ]

# Fetching Fats From Urupunga Station to Katherine Meatworks

This is a country of rushes and ringing in,
Of clean-skins and bang-tailed musters,
Of hunting strays from the shrinking waters
Of the smell of leather and horses and diesel
Of yard gates closed and road trains rolling up.

This is a country of scrub bulls and trap cattle,
Of endless plains and dead-end tracks
Where insignificance rolls onwards and forward
Under red dust through sparse scrub
And the rigs will find their station late of day.

This is a country where the land falls away
Behind the horizon as the brutal sun
Glows ochre-daubed and heat glimmered
At close of play and the loading ramp goes quiet
And the driver checks tires and couplings

This is a country where stock is broken
And those untamed are fenced and penned
And even the wildest from the bush runs

Are lulled by rubbing girths and stifles
As the road train runs on into the night

Come the deepest dark the lights shine out
Across the red country and its dusty trails
Into the black soil plains, fighting for the hard top,
Culvert by culvert, marker by marker flash-lighting
Tremors and shadows from the convoy.

Hands too tired and lips too dry to seal a roll-your-own,
Come the dawn and the bitumen straight as a die
Leads on to Katherine, stun gun and skinning knife:
This is a land of small and very grudging mercies
With no holds barred on driving hell for leather.

---

Keith Johnson is a semi-retired Development Economist from Wellington, NZ who worked across the world but grew up in the English countryside as the stepson of a Cheshire farmer. Allpoetry.com/Keith_Johnson

[ Steven Gress ]

# Fall's Victim

brittle,
like leaves in December,
dried by the crisp air.
You fall away in pieces
with the veins exposed.

kissed madness,
veiled by the grey skies
and peach cobbler sunsets
a thousand deaths
riddled by affinity.

evoking cobwebs,
splintered by cardinal wings.
A splash of color echoes
falsely to the laughing moon.
Seeing you as you are.

Blindsided by betrayal,
a victim of the fall.

---

Living in Wesley Chapel Fl. Been writing poetry on and off for plus 40 years. Poetry is a stress therapy for me. Allpoetry.com/Agressman

[ Joseph John Taras Kushnir ]

# Gathered In a Piney Circle

Snowy white falls outside
the house hushed with
wintery respect.

An orange glow paints
the frosted window,
amber light matted on chilled concern.

Inside the wide dining room
eyes gaze wide as a quiet yule reflection
is pondered by the young and old.

Purple candles gathered around
in a piney green circle,
prayers countdown the Messiah's birth.

---

I'm a painter/writer/martial arts teacher from Bayonne New Jersey. Creativity and it's manifestation has always been an essential part of me, and I always delight in bringing my zany outlook to others. Allpoetry.com/Joseph_Kushnir

[ Jon Richards ]

# View from Carn Brea

This long ridged hill with granite outcrops
Crowned at its top, by a massive stone cross
Looks down past my hometown, on to the Atlantic
Surging restless beneath the skies vast horizon.

Looking out to the west, near 30 miles distant
St.Ives white houses nestled under a dark headland
Away in the background, stand the purple hills of Penwith
So often hidden by shrouded sea mist.

Here is a world modelled in miniature
Tiny houses surrounded by patchwork fields
And always blue sea, and the tall cliffs of Cornwall
At the border of this green realm.

The sunset settles into the western sea
Inflaming the waves in shades of crimson
The skies silver expanse, speaks of mystery
While the scarlet sun sinks down to Avalon.

40 years old. Been writing for 2 years now. Living in Cornwall. I enjoy descriptive poetry. Trying to convey some of the beauty around me. Allpoetry.com/Escaped_Poet

[ David I Mayerhoff ]

# Cold Contrasts

The snowman
was well placed by the kids
in the yard
greeting all passers- by

Cold temperatures outside
descended well below freezing
with ice shards
growing down
over the windows

Our exhaling breath blew
smoke
as if the lungs
were on fire

Yet inside
it was warm to the touch
as we awoke in the morning
heat on and under the blankets

Watching the great frost out there
and soaking in the delightful warmth in here
created a stimulating contrast

that magnified

the totality of our raw pleasure

well above what we could enjoy

experiencing the cold or the warmth alone

---

David I Mayerhoff is a newly emerging writer while being a practicing physician and psychiatrist for the last 34 years. Allpoetry.com/David_Mayerhoff

[ Danielle Linggar ]

# The Sun Rises in the East

Effulgent semi-circle peers timorously,
intervening subtle grassy horizons
as it crawls up the quartz-clear sky
tittle-by-tittle by the minute.

Ambrosial sun bestirs mundane creatures
from their evening slumber
with its tender light, a silent hum
of an archaic hymn.

The radiant sphere hovers at
rose-violet candy floss dawn,
its genial yellow hue sweet
as saccharine lemon drops.

The aroma of budding sunshine
is like a garden of Dutch daffodils
that tickles inside your nose
with its mellow, fragrant kisses.

Gilded rays trickle through
ethereal whipped cream clouds
to waltz on your skin with their
dainty, microscopic ballerina legs.

---

Danielle Linggar is from Jakarta, Indonesia. Poetry helps me cope with boredom and tough times. I like playing the piano in my spare time. Allpoetry.com/Danielle_L.

[ Lawrence Mosieri ]

# Disney Springs Is Come Of Age

Heaven's gates burst
open, letting out gust

of angels led by Cherubim
and Seraphim, all with a beam

of smiles and a light in hand,
whence shinning Disney sky dome heralded

Disney Springs is come of age.
Guests stood in awe and page

blossoming planters leaf
tenderly, while angels rejoiced in disbelief!

See now, the craft of doodle burger and shine,
the ringing tone of COOP Guest shopping dime,

that bears semblance of performance
and excellence, all in evidence.

───────────

My name is Lawrence Mosieri, from Milwaukee, Wisconsin. Poetry is for brilliant minds. I have the ambition of become a published Poet. Pound is my Hero. Allpoetry.com/Lawrence_Mosieri

[ Lisa O' Mahony ]

# The Man in the Attic

With the blitheness of the day,
I begin folding pristine clean clothes away.

When distance drones command my consciousness,
My inquisitiveness draws heed from me,
Unstirring,
A cold chill waltzes over me.

Momentarily reminded,
It's the man in the attic.

Shifting his torso around the wooden beam,
He has awakened from his supernatural sleep.
Invisible to the naked eye,
his existence is hard to predict.

His beady eyes follow you,
Watching you tentatively,
Through every nook and cranny,
Keyholes and jarred floor boards.

Eerily reminding you of his present,
By shape shifting around,

At the witching hour of night.

I have never met the man in the attic,
But I know he exists.

―――――――――――

I am a novice writer. I did the Artist's way recently and started painting and writing poetry. I live in a small town by the sea called Balbriggan near Dublin, Ireland. I have a passion for writing. Allpoetry.com/Lis_O_Mahony

[ Samantha Cheshire ]
# Fleeting Affections

gracefully, she sweeps the veil across

her plum-blushed cheeks, whilst gazing

upon her smouldering reflection

his words are taken, smuggled from

glistening lips, his mind pivots,

plunging deeper into her gaze

as she whispers the revelations

of the stars, his face lights up,

baring a smile which hungers for more

he tries to hold in his naked

emotions, yet they become drunk,

stumbling into her beckoning arms.

suddenly, the hand of an enchanter

wraps his cloak around her shoulders, putting

an end to this newly birthed romance

---

Samantha currently resides in her county of birth, Shropshire, England. She has been writing since 2014. Apart from writing, her other passions include studying the Bible and keeping fit. Allpoetry.com/Burning_Rose

[ Maxwell E. Hoover ]

# swimming

overalls and sloppy kisses.
running barefoot - don't blink.
there goes
your childhood.

acne and cowlicks.
piercing crushes and sharpie markers.
lockers, drama, and judgement.

study hard
or you'll never
be a man.

slam your foot down
on the pedal.
roll the window down and don't forget to sing.

foul mouth and
black lungs.
just keep swimming.
you're a man now.

———————

Max is a passionate student and outdoorsman from NE Ohio. He is working on publishing his first book, sincerely yours. He is a certified PADI scuba diver and Eagle Scout. allpoetry.com/meh595 Allpoetry.com/meh595

[ Celeste Jackson ]

# Take Your Pamphlets Somewhere Else

You sting
my eyes
sometimes,

with that
white square,
10-am-sun-
off-hot-window-glass
brilliance.

I know
we're supposed
to strive for
excellence,
thrust ourselves
over proverbial
cliffs
and soar
into the distance,
little dandelion
seeds
full of potential,

but while you
were adding
feathers
to your quivering wings
I filled
my pockets
with uneven
stones
and prepared myself
for the
plummet.

I don't want
to sail into sunsets
and blue skies,
just for
Truman Show
walls
to bust
my bow,

I would rather
sink
to grey shores
and line my
stones
along the

water's edge,

build myself
a rough rock
tower,
and steel
its lumbering bones
against the
flow
you keep
badgering me
to go with.

I would rather
bust
the panes
from my castle
windows,
and let the heat
touch dull floors
uninterrupted,

feel the
scrape
of warm cut earth
beneath my feet
and struggle

up the stairs
I carved
myself
through
the painted
ceiling,

than leap
into your watercolor
wind
and find myself
bleeding.

Maybe
I am hard
and cold
and boring
and my salt
chafes your
soft flesh,

but when you
are rocking
in pastel puddles
among bigger
waves,
it will be
my

grey rain

that floods

the sea.

———————

Celeste Jackson is an upstart writer from a small town in southern Missouri currently fumbling her way through life on the East Coast. She spends her days writing and annoying her wonderful husband. Allpoetry.com/Teyana_Celeste

[ Chelsea Rainford ]

# Finnimbrun

Six fingered hands on akimbo wrists
cover my blindfolded lids,
three layers between
the greyscale landscapes
and my field-colour eyes.

I am swathed in rainy days
and cloud cover but feel
the sun beating beneath
my ribs and breast—

almost extinguished
by damp knapweed-stippled wool.

---

Chelsea Rainford grew up in suburbs along Lake Ontario, caught between a chaotic city and dwindling farmland. That contrast, combined with her unique perspective, expresses itself in all her poetry. Allpoetry.com/C._E._Rainford

[ Aditya Rao ]

# The Sun

So wild and wide-eyed, where windy and warm,
   Soaked in the metronome of ocean-foam
Where igneous petals and cinders swarm
   And wake the molten medal in its home.

But below the shallow shimmer and show
   Hides but a sum most untidy to claim—
Hardly two cents' worth—a cobblestone's throw
   To add to my inestimable name.

---

Aditya Rao is from Dade City, Florida, and has been writing poetry since high school. It has been a serious passion. Allpoetry.com/Aditya_Rao

[ Rachael S. Mcdermott ]

# footslog

Flee for home as a west wind blows,
like a prey spots the dreadful hawks.
Then, all at once go numb my toes,
and bones vibrate like bamboo stalks.
Ears and nose are a little dead,
and this coat is no warming bed.

In flurries and chills below eight,
I trudge over piles mounting high
along the stretch by every gate.
No signs of life, no passersby
in these flakes - confetti air raid -
that fly in fast like fusillade.

I hear the crush each shoe makes
between the wind's howling sounds.
My teeth chatter, I have the shakes,
and ankle deep in snowy mounds.
All clad in white that's heaven sent,
I tough out my predicament.

Six blocks alone, but sure prevail,
as the last block home gets easy.
Alas, recall tonight's long travail

in central heat, warm and cozy.
While nature rages on outside,
a sigh of relief cheers inside.

———————

An up-and-coming poet who lives in Queens, NY United States; born in Kingston, Jamaica. One published work, God, Loves & Me© - 2016 ISBN: 978-1-52450-305-5 Allpoetry.com/EmpressRachyMc

[ Alona Perlin ]

# The Joy of Winter

Crackling fire
Falling flakes
What a pretty scene this makes

Leaves are rustling on the ground
Nothing nearby makes a sound

Lighted candles on the hearth
People full of joy and mirth
Pets are resting safe inside
From the storm they're trying to hide

While the wind is howling by
And there's turmoil in the sky

We must stay in our retreat
Heads on winter, we will meet!

---

Alona Perlin is a poet, classical pianist and social worker. She resides in Brooklyn, N.Y. with her beloved dog, Princess! Allpoetry.com/APerlin

[ Winter Kage ]
# Silent

I cannot hear the wind today
No cricket sings sweet melodies
Birds are silent in the trees
The reeds are quite bent

Stepping on cement beneath my feet
wait patiently for an echo
that never comes
Children do not laugh or call
as they play
Traffic passes
without a screech, honk
or motorized hum

At the cafe on the corner
vibrations from the band
jar my bones
in silent air
I want a particular song
feeling it will be enough
but the ink of my note fades
I have no way to ask for it

The waitress looks expectant
lips never part
My mouth moves
issuing mute words
I must point to my choice, but
pages have been torn from my book

Fireworks light the sky
no familiar bang follows
and I wonder who
celebrates this deaf world?

Soundless sobs wrack my chest
I would give anything
for a bit of noise
the chirp of a cricket
serenade of a bird
laughter of children, or at least
the words to make it happen

---

Kage is from Morehead, Kentucky. Has been a writer since he was in Middle school. Became a musician in High School and now is the primary lyricist for his own band. Allpoetry.com/WinterKage

[ Alwyn Barddylbach ]

# Enchanted

Whispers light upon my desk wilful spun, again
flickered wings dancing to long grain shadows,
tinderbox of embers gold in autumn sun.

Far, far away the world that was the day is over,
in absent twilight sacred flame remember,
fly, fly beyond the setting sun playful tell her.

Evening fades the crimson firefly shines on,
many minds comb the secret stars at night
chasing brief moments in faithful freedom.

Enchanted spell, o tiny sun-kissed lantern
shine brighter now than any wish might forge and
playful tell her the day remembered -
it's a glorious one.

---

'Whisper her name softly again' says Barddylbach in the Kata Tjuta sunset, 'begin wherever you wish and she will be enchanted' - Postcard from Alice. Allpoetry.com/Barddylbach

[ Kaylie Rosenberry ]

# Shadow On the Snow

Grey, the early dawn
That fades out the color of midnight
Grey the light that filters in through closed curtains
And pools on the floor like fog

Grey the years have drained you
The color not quite as bright
And you not quite as sprightly
As you used to be

Grey eyes that swallow the light
And reflect it back in silver sheen
Grey the depths of liquid smoke
That draw me in to drown and sing

Grey the hills that stretch out
Far beyond my reach
Grey the distance that I cannot cover
To stand on your distant shores

Grey the silence that covers the sea
Beneath a sky white and cold
Grey the waves that pulsate
Thick and shifting in fading night

Grey the whisper that echoes in your mind
The dream of years that once shone
Now dull and faded with time
Grey is for their memory as your weary head bows

Grey the earth where nature endlessly toils
Who gives its life to fill the needs
Of others breathing above and below
Grey death's shadow as it lays upon the snow

---

Kaye Rose has been a prolific poet and fantasy writer for many years. Her writing is inspired by Tolkien, Robert Frost, C.S. Lewis, and the intense beauty of life and emotion itself. Allpoetry.com/Kaye_Rose

[ Simona Prilogan ]

# Seeking my own

Empty-headed I was running
hungry to catch the morning rays,
empowering my sight and tuning
I'm on my innocence's ways.

I took the hint of flowers smiles,
of shadow lights on evening hour.
I watched the moon behind of eyes
of inner mind on darkness power.

I laughed while dancing with the Sun,
I washed the tears in rain, alone.
Today more empty-handed than
Before, I'm still seeking my own...

---

I have been writing poetry all my life, in my native language - Romanian. 4 years ago I have started learning English on my own, and 1 year later I wrote my first English poem. This one. Allpoetry.com/Simona_Prilogan

[ Trudi Ruth Benford ]

# Thirst

And in the end,
I married the good one.

My big white car never has
a burned out bulb for long.

Security wraps my almost-grown daughter,
tucked nightly into bed by a safe man.

My son learns algebra without me,
beyond my care, or knowing.

Bedtime at ten, dog twice-walked,
fall leaves raked, woodpile neat.

Wine organized and chilled,
even the reds so they keep longer.

Sometimes I long for a warm pour
straight from the bottle.

---

Through her poetry, Trudi explores the complexities of connectedness and longing. With incisive language, she shines a light on love: unrequited, obsessive, nostalgic or reciprocated. Allpoetry.com/Takoma

[ Tracy Banks ]

# Fire

Fatal with wind;
totally hot! Roaming for food with forceful inhalation
and exhalation.

Shifting moods
spreading huge symbols over the wind.
Evil and bright,
leaving it's burnt offerings behind.

Across the land an empty address book.
I cavort with desirous curtains of rain;
fire is in thrall with water
relief!

---

I am from Brooklyn Park, MN and my hobbies are reading and writing poetry. I love poetry because it's a beautiful language. It's also changed my perception and now I see symbolism everywhere. Allpoetry.com/Tracybanks65

[ Kevin Mathew Panackal ]

# Mind Street

pale colors
drip onto canvas
via my tensions
they travel

upon the white
flat field
and make scars
of blue

crystalline patches
grow from
the pot of
yearning dreams

for those which try
to break that
chandelier,
'I will paint them black'.

I'm driving out of
fused confusion
laying head on
grey pillow cases.

Kevin Mathew Panackal son of Shibu Mathew and Jasmin Mathew was born in New York, USA but moved to Kerala, India when he was four years old. 'Poetry has a really therapeutic effect, it empowers me'.
Allpoetry.com/Diamond_Mist

[ Dylan Church ]

# Ballroom of Blisters

Our sundown brother
son of the sikhs and the monsoon metropolis.
Impaled by loyalty to a fool
with illuminated fingertips
like a deep marine siren.
Dancing her charming lantern
with toxic intentions.
A communion through friendly
needles, itching
for a taste of virgin venation
and plump passages.
Brought to bloom by a colorful cruelty,
boiled into tranquility
to slither red pearls;
crimson messengers
that guide the blight, a river miasma
to sooth the nimble nucleus.
A deluge of booze and heroin disturbs
your visceral harmony,
driving brilliant scarlet to frightened cavities.
Swollen and flavescent
trembling on the carpet like a newborn widow.
Boiling tears as hot as the vomit

sizzling on your chest
cascade down your cheeks,
as you long for your mother
and her comfort.
Before your eyes
turn to spheres of crystalline.
Fluttered fingers
sticky and swift
pummel your ribcage;
the drumfire gates to reclaim
that thermal tremor,
from the placid cadence its come to be.
Your departure left our bodies
perverted in despondency
like curling leaves,
mangled by that cold autumn anchor.
Saturated palms,
littered upon our crowning star.
Your once inky figure
now a mass of porcelain instruments.
We dig our nails in your flesh
to scar our goodbyes,
to ensure the imprint
of our sonnetts in the paling stream
of electricity.
Denying our hearts the wisdom
of your lonely descent, beneath the tombstone prairie.

Will keep your image evergreen,

free from the worms

and the smoldering leaves,

where only shriveled silhouettes survive.

———————

My name is dylan church and I'm from bellingham washington. I'm a junior at western washington university pursuing my bachelors in English/creative writing. Allpoetry.com/Slowdive45

[ Lesly Frances Finn ]

# The Ball Gown

the girl in the mirror stands high on tip-toe
she arches her back as she's tying the bow
at the back of the dress, then starts doing a twirl
turning this way and that, the skirts billow and swirl

such a beautiful dress, it belonged to her mother
so carefully kept and loved as no other
the girl closes her eyes and imagines the dance
in the arms of a lover, the start of romance

moving daintily now as she hums out the tune
she goes twirling and swirling around the bedroom
while just for the moment she is there in her place
and with nobody watching she waltzes with grace

---

Lesly is English but has lived in New Zealand since 1999. She has always loved drawing and painting, also music and reading, and has now found an affinity to writing poetry. Allpoetry.com/LeslyF

[ Sarah Gosa ]

# Grand Isle

The river road would bend and
curve and we would climb and
fall with the resistance of a
warm milkshake travelling through
a swivel straw. Foreshadowing:
the ferry's loll sleep then wake
in an upside-down town where
we'd watch the ships rise from
bone. In the heat of melting
iron on a shore of lace strewn
scallops, embedded in the oily
sand souring in a pan of fried
sun whelped day and the night
was a gang of hermits clamping
sharp on our shard-bitten barefeet.

---

Sarah Gosa is from Fort Smith, Arkansas. I enjoy spending time with my family, hiking, drawing, writing and an occasional wild goose chase. Allpoetry.com/Sarah_Gosa

[ Gc Basher ]

# Finely Crafted Ending

Our cars pulled in among the trees
and rows of chiseled stone –
so orderly, a place prepared for us,
like everything was in – control.
A breeze made its own path,
nudging the pines from their nap
as his grandsons helped to lug
the finely crafted box
where it would drop
when we left.

I was left to say the Final Words
that didn't end a damn thing –
not the questions,
not the raging sorties from hearts to souls.
Some words hit the box with a thud.
Others tripped over themselves
running away from our hearts.
Even the breeze couldn't wait,
stepping over us on the way out,
and the venerable pines slipped back to sleep.

Currently residing in Dover, Delaware, GC Basher is a former teacher of American Literature and language arts who has studied and written poetry over a span of four decades. Allpoetry.com/G_C_Basher

[ Bianca Szasz ]

# Jokes

I painted my room
With the blood of drunk lovers
And I mixed the sunset colors
With the pitch of a walking dead.

The marbled sun
Drowned into the river...
Stunning view
Of a dead woman kissing a rose.

Cursed with empty memories,
Your life is not free.
I bought it for a silver treasure,
Buried under Death's tree.

The sun will soon lay down on you
With all his life's philosophy...
The Sufi poet is now telling jokes
Instead of writing poetry.

---

Bianca Szasz is a Romanian space enthusiast, living in Japan. Self-inquiry, intergalactic travels and searching for ultimate truths are some of her interests. Allpoetry.com/Proxima_B

[ Finbarr Harkin ]

# Poseidon's Beasts

Born of the wind these ocean swells,
within the power of nature dwells;
Poseidon's beasts come out to play,
Immense in power and might they sway.

With churning heave they show their heads,
these roaring, trashing white loc dreads,
and foaming mouth with gnashers bare,
inviting death to those who dare.

Upon the battered shore they smash,
and there with venom skyward crash;
the air it thick with hazy brine,
as on the land with hunger dine.

As wind dies down the master calls,
upon the seas a calmness falls;
no evidence of frenzied feast,
the wildest tempest now has ceased.

---

Finbarr Harkin is from Donegal in Ireland, he grew up in a small fishing village and has a fascination and love for the power of nature especially costal/sea related

which is reflected in his poetry. Allpoetry.com/
Finbarr_Harkin

[ Sujata Baruah ]

# My Sweet Valentine

In my silence of the solitude,
I once began to hear a melody,
calling me from the distant woods,

Our eyes met,
bewiched by a tinge of
charming tenderness!

Softly and gently
flowed an ecstasy
in the song.

Now glowing like embers
in the dark, my sweet Valentine.

Fondling and embracing
in each other's arms,
our eyes closing
to kiss, like roses red,
apple of my eyes.

Breaking the rules and bonds
of the shackles of the world,
together we burn like a flame
yellow as honey and red as wine

to kindle in ourselves a feeling

of sweet togetherness.

---

I am from India. Writing poetry gives me immense pleasure to pursue as a hobby. I find it quite interesting since it enables me to spend my leisure hours fruitfully. Allpoetry.com/Sujata_Baruah

[ Estella Sanders ]

# Ohio State University

My heart goes out to Ohio State University
The Injuries and harm that was Caused by
An unknown individual, Continue
Living in Sins of this world,
Family member of Students,
You are in my prayers

---

Reading these poems will give you understanding and knowledge who Jesus Christ is and his good works. Jesus created this world and gave us all life that we all shall live and be fruitful. Allpoetry.com/Esfrenchholyje

[ Drew Lagoon ]
# Bone Breathing

Our skeletons are antennas
Channeling energies to sustain us
And I feel your presence with each breath
It's burning through
An ocean of calmness

Everything is misshapen
End over end tumbling
Gracelessly
Through our meridians
And our balance is flawed
Yet
Determinate we swim on the floor
Eyes fixed on the mesmerizing wave

It is internalizing
But there is a oneness that exists
Embracing the tree
And I feel a forgotten happiness
As the knot unties itself

Drew is from Southern Georgia. Writing certainly helps me untie those knots that are borne of fear and anxiety. It's very cathartic in nature. And when I put that writing to song, it is truly alive. Allpoetry.com/Mysterier

[ Kyle Schlicher ]

# Quaaludes And Nyquil

time was
the world made perfectly good sense.

way back
when the menu
read
such as thus:

take one brown bottle of rorer 714's,

no one cares,
the passing lane is empty,
take as many
as needed
and
then more.

wash them down with the contents
of the green bottle
and
sit back
and
wait.

and the world
did
make perfectly good sense;

a self prescribed

prescription
for self hallucinating dreams
of the wandering madman
turning away
and

the empty green bottle
falling
to the floor,

slowly.......rolling......down

the
darkened hallway.

soon, comes crashing waves
of
welcomed opiate likeness
as the fingers
and

lips

grew increasingly numb

and

time

appeared

to be

breathing

slowly

with

each

passing

second

feeling

like a year

of the sentence

handed down by yourself;

and that

one

mindless mistaken moment

you

made the choice

to open

the cookie jar.

---

I live in Gulfport, Florida. I make a daily attempt to write and I have in my possession the one and only original Bullwinkle Leaf. Allpoetry.com/Slickone

[ Patricia A Edwards ]

# Just Beyond my Touch

Just beyond my reach
I saw you there, I felt your touch
you caressed my hair
you stood beyond my fingertips

I was standing alone in the darkness there
did you really come back to me
or was it just a state outside of me
as you stood just beyond my fingertips.

---

I am from Masury, Ohio, and use poetry as a way of expressing my inner self and coping with my feelings. I feel that if I can help one person cope, then I've achieved my goal. Allpoetry.com/Sweetlady53

[ Stephen Jackson ]

# Inheritance

Growing up
My father was a shadow
In the shade cast
A weight was passed
Down to me,
Unconsciously.

Treasured it must be
to carry something
precious and heavy;
tattered
like a cherished family recipe.

I waited for colour
To fill the lack
But nothing appeared
So I painted pictures
Of an ideal man
With hopeful strokes
of distorted fancy.

Now forgiven
like a recessive gene,
knowing how the mind

stretches from the past

To the present

Filling gaps left by absence.

With no son

To pass the weight on

It will implode,

Silently,

Inside me,

Like a lonely sun in a far off galaxy.

But my inheritance

Can still be fatherly

With words written carefully

So another man's wait

May not feel so heavy.

---

Stephen Jackson is from London, UK and has been writing and performing poetry for the last year. Topics cover identity and masculinity affecting the modern gay man. Allpoetry.com/Stephen_Jackson

[ Nicholas 'Georgie' Scott ]

# Somewhere In The Attic

At the bottom of the toy box
and the last thing on his mind
buried deep beneath his passions
without his love or time

Longing for his approval
to walk his joyful way
to be in his box of treasure
that he opens everyday

Somewhere in the attic
in a box faded by time
emotions left unspoken
not yours or hers but mine

---

I'm transgendered, male to female - I appear as male but my personality is female. Georgie is my female name. My interests include cosmology and science. I live in the UK, and was born in 1961. Allpoetry.com/Nicholas_Scott

[ Bharati Nayak ]

# A Tree I Am

I look at you

In pure amazement

Like a tree

I stand in silence

Though in excitement

I shiver

I lack words

My emotions are an ocean

You greet me

As the first ray

of sunlight

I enliven

My branches swing

As if to touch you

Inside me

I am flowering

My moment comes

When you come near me

Stand in my shade

We breathe together

When song birds sing

And the wind murmurs

Born on 26th may 1962 in Odisha, India, Bharati Nayak grew up in Cuttack and graduated from the famous Ravenshaw College. Allpoetry.com/Bharati1962

[ Paul Hernandez ]

# Silent Light

In my mind I hear what I want to say,
the words form but I can't say
what I'm thinking.

There's a room at the end of hall
where all is hidden inside.
There's a sliver of light
that glows at the bottom of the door.

Now and then she comes to the room
but doesn't enter, no, she will not open the door.
She try's to speak but sound has eluded her.

Slowly her head hangs low, she turns and walks away,
her fingers drag behind on the knob as she
gently releases it from her grasp.

Is it all for me, a room filled full of emptiness?
The desire is there but I can't touch what I am feeling,
my eyes see the beam of light, the only thing I can see.
I don't know where I am!

Once again she finds herself standing at
the door to the room at the end of the hall.

Hope is the light that shines forth
from the other side of the door.

Loooking away only for a moment,
for fear she might miss seeing a shadow pass,
a sign that there's life beyond her silence.

Her head hangs low and tears
begin to flow, beading down her face.

The hand of courage
turns the knob pushing forward
she steps into the sound of her voice,
the light beyond the door at the end of the hall.

---

Born January 15 1971 in Los Angeles, CA. Raised in Bell CA. Writing has become my outlet, I love writing exactly how I'm feeling in that very moment so I can capture that emotional portrait in words. Allpoetry.com/PaulyWally

[ Terence M Sheppard ]
# Amongst the cold and the grey

Amongst the cold and the grey,
the bricks, the wires, the chimney stacks.
The heavy gloom, the pouring rain,
the feel of night, although it is day.

Amongst the cold and the grey,
here where time stands still.
There stretches a landscape of death,
no blossoms, no blooms, no sweet bouquet.

Amongst the cold and the grey,
demons in corners still dwell.
Amidst this cacophony of silence,
upon the conscious of men they play.

Amongst the cold and the grey,
forlorn, the figures looking back at me.
Abandoned in stripes of black and white,
human beings in a state of decay.

Amongst the cold and the grey,
Stares fraught with terror and loss.
Captured forever to ruminate,
these bodies as moulded from potters clay.

Amongst the cold and the grey
I walk the path millions have taken.
Along time ago, a time now passed,
yet forgotten belongings here still stay.

Amongst the cold and the grey,
sunny afternoons and long beach walks.
Love and happiness with holding hands,
forever lost these memories of a happier day.

Amongst the cold and the grey,
children who skipped and played.
Who laughed and loved,
had their innocence taken away.

Amongst the cold and the grey,
red dye does retain its colour.
Amidst these relics of a wicked past,
best Sunday shoes now lay.

Amongst the cold and the grey,
someone left alone in darkness to stand.
Shoulders touching the walls of rooms
with no freedom to kneel and pray.

Amongst the cold and the grey,
children clutching hands so tight.

Crystals of tiny blue,
a shower of vapour to end their day.

Amongst the cold and the grey
I see a father, a mother with children stand.
I see the spray that covers the wall,
I feel the rain try and wash it away.

Amongst the cold and the grey
a quiet guilt does haunt this place.
For here a factory processed evil,
while a nation went quietly about its day.

Amongst the cold and the grey
I feel the lingering of those long gone.
A connection with me there is none,
yet a guilt upon my conscience does weigh.

Amongst the cold and the grey
now stands this monument to human depravity.
Where humanity comes face to face
with its ultimate capacity for evil....decay

Amongst the cold and the grey
I cannot help but have thought of home.
Where fear and hate are dangerously fuelled.

Could we see this horror again someday?

Terence Sheppard is from the UK. Poetry is a way for me to express those feelings and thoughts that are generated everyday via life's experiences. Allpoetry.com/Terence_Sheppard

[ Gregory Francis Schrupp ]
# Empty air of butterfly sunshine II

Fragile air floats free,
wing'ed breath beats heart rhythm
caught by searching sky.
Sails, colored whispers in tide,
afloat, yesterday's mem'ries.

Melody monarch
sings sadness of moment's flight
Her song carries swift
through day's breezy flow.
Season colors adorn her.

Butterfly sunshine
strikes eagle's eye of wonder,
as mind ascends heights.
Airborne souls costumed by time
and infinite need of change.

Disappear dreams, die,
to reflections pondered true,
reborn as child's mind.
Soft silk surrounds the sensual
escaping death's dilemma.

Pen name is the Jester Prince. Poetry and creative writing expanded my universe. It is a powerful tool in thought and idea, one that has changed me. I love the dark, the erotic and the fantastical. Allpoetry.com/Jester_Prince

[ Catherine Welch ]

# Untitled first post

All the dishes I do

All the beds that I make .

It makes it worth

every breath that I take.

When I turn off the lights

The voices I hear

in the still of the night

that are so dear

    "I love you too, mommy."

———————

I wrote this years ago for my kids and now I have the pleasure of sharing this with my grandchildren, I am so blessed. Thank you for publishing. Allpoetry.com/Gmacato123

[ Andy Sprouse ]

# Silence and Solemnity of Snow

There's a silence and solemnity to snow -
a sacredness in the soft folds of winter's gleaming cloak.

It was there when last love cast away from me,
when it found me once more in the boughs behind my home.
Alone inside the house before, I raged, I writhed,
unsure of who I was or what followed.

In those branches my tears and cries froze, silenced,
in the stillness of a white hand gently fallen on my shoulder.
Countless soft fingertips landed on me and 'round,
windlessly drifting down, soothing without wintry bite.

A broken heart it had not the power to mend,
simply lull for a few moments in time;
providing succor enough for contemplation, thought,
rather than screaming for what was thrown away.

It wasn't there for years while away in warm places,
and perchance those years have been the most chaotic;
the tune of the island upbeat, not sedate,
the hush of the jungle a threat, not a solace.

Mayhap when this upheaval has been put to rest,
so too will my hiatus from chill's cotton calm.
Mayhap I'll climb the trees of the past,
and in the flurries and flakes see a future.

There's a silence and solemnity to snow -
a smile hidden in the cold, in the white, in the magic.

---

Andy Sprouse is a young musician and writer, just recently returned to southern Maryland from a few years of traveling. Like many, poetry is his way of thinking out loud, of sharing his experiences. Allpoetry.com/wolfdrummer13

[ Tina King ]

# I want to be the sunbeam

I love the way the sunlight
shines in through the window blinds
accentuating the softest part of you

I love how music moves you,
How each note
resonates
Deep
Inside

And you sway to the beat
like a sapling
in the summer breeze

I love the way the water
Envelopes you
Reaching every crevice-
all your freckles,
dimples,
and scars

I want to be the sunbeam
and your favorite song,
the forest floor

beneath your feet,

and the water

in which you drown.

---

I live in the mid-west but love to travel wherever the wind may blow. I enjoy live music and outdoor activities. I find poetic inspiration in the beautiful world around me & from the people I love. Allpoetry.com/Tina_King

[ George Robinson ]
# At The Beach

Relucent dunes, gulls and the deep blue brine
Sea breezes rustling beachgrass glance my face
Return to tidal land my nature pines
Jejune recalls without a single trace

Rank trawlers, smelly bait, and tidal mud
The foul cues which unseal the vault of truth
A paper mill repugnance marks my blood
The Southern sun exposes absent youth

The images of my inner eye are cloaked
and they are haunting me like ghosts in lies
A wish for history but none evoked
In trauma versus will, will always dies

No childhood to recall I find in my gloom
Bedimmed as pictures in a sunny room

———————

I've been writing in one form or another since my early teens. I discovered poetry is my true milieu. Allpoetry.com/Pentimento

[ Ludvig Hoel ]

# Onward bound we go

The wind blows.
A storm is coming.
It is downwind and we set sail.

Onward bound we go.

The sea is roaring.
A darkness cloaks our bearing.
The wrath of Neptune comes our way.

Onward bound we go.

The sky is glowing.
We fear nothing
and will prevail!

Onward bound we go.

---

Im a student of Bsc in law and Bsc in Energy Managent. I needed a hobby, and have always read books and poems, så it was a easy choice. Poems is a great way to express feelings or make stories true. Allpoetry.com/GinToxic

[ Mary Beth Holland ]

# Taste the Amber

Clarity shines through
a cloudy consumption
of introverted happiness,
soaking
in the last hour of warmth
upon this front porch
of reason.

Thirsty for the chill
of nightfall.

---

Mary Beth is a mother of three amazing children from Waynesboro, VA. She began writing while being a stay at home mom, and has now become one of her favorite hobbies. Allpoetry.com/Dee_White

[ Ritika Singh ]

# I Pray

I pray,

may your eye-liner never smudge

may your eyes always shine

may your lipstick keep passing on to other cheeks

and your heels and standards be high

may you be the light in the dark

and your lashes never turn down

and your heels never stop tik tok

and they'll keep making this sound

may the places where you walk

you keep spreading the smell of rose

I hope the people to whom you talk

keep saying you're perfect from head to toe!

---

Ritika Singh is from GZB, India,she is 14 years old and she is a keyboardist, sings, and writing is in her blood. Enjoy my poems! I love the person who is reading this! Allpoetry.com/Ritika1705

[ Allison W ]

# The Lady in Blue

She wove and waved the silk in the meadow,
Where she flattened her petticoat, expression as low.
Her pen markings have flown to the young man downtown,
The place where she sent her laughter into the chimney's smoke.

Beneath her petticoat, a little rhythm you hear,
The blue rhinestones stepping and humming in the mist.
She has a kettle heart that steams that too pours,
But those that know cannot hear,
Because she has stopped it every time for the ones she endears.

Nobody really knows where the petticoat has gone this year,
For they have lost patience and grown a new fear.
The woven silk has been too long a mystery,
For they have ignored for too long,
And the war soldiers stopped the retreats.

Maybe someday when the meadow has faded,
She shall vanish, without a word of what she did,
And perhaps renew the dark forest.

The birds chirp once more,
With the trees waltzing for much to adore.
For in the meadows beneath the forest,
A new life dancing in the rain, I see.

Forever more shall I remember the lady with the blue rhinestones,
The one who wove the silk in the meadow.
For shall I leave for the last time,
To let her grace remain a secret.
To come back home without a word,
For the secret only I know must remain only mine.

---

Allison is from California. I like to write poetry whenever I have a strong feeling, whether negative or positive. Allpoetry.com/AmityHeart

[ Astrid Tejero ]

# One Love, Two Souls Equally Yoked

A night past dawn, dressed in white in a vintage floral purple Antoinette Apron, her hair volumptious with curls above her shoulder's.

She stand in the kitchen, before the stove, her arms in length maneuvering as she prepared supper.

Turmoil came across the room while little children amusingly play. She veer with joy and ponder their innocence.

Her luminous radiance shined from where she stand, her smile reflected the pureness of a virtuous woman.

Blessed is she for her meekness and obedience.

She strides towards her sturdy dining table, fixing two places with white fine-line silver splendor plates and allure stainless glossy forks on the side.

Suddenly, she perks up and appraises with joy a fine, handsome, sophisticated tall man, strong, and slim fit.

He is dressed in white, his point collar shirt unbutton, he weard black cashmere pants, his coat hung from one arm and a suitcase from the other.

Her beloved has finally arrived home. In constrain to hold his beloved he placed everything above the rustic bench next to the dinner table.

Both his arms reached her waist, imbued he gaze at her in astonishment.

For a moment their world stop to turned as both scrutinized one another.

He did not kiss her before his meal, he sat on the verge of the bench and commenced his dinner.

Once his meal concluded,
he turned to open one leg outside the bench,
"would you join me?" he told his beloved.

She rested in between his chest while he wrapped his arms around her.

In whispers to her ear,
his voice deep and angelic he said,
"how was your day my love?"

She replied, "a day of victory and rejoice."

He smiled in delight with her response.
"honey you know I love you right?
tell me what are you feeling?"

She shook her head indeed for the mutual feeling.
Then softly he kissed her on the side of her cheek.

Both admire one another,
their love was pure, clean and honest.
No one could set them apart but God.

---

Astrid Tejero is from California a young mom of two, woman of faith, christian worship singer. A full time Aerospace buyer, part time College Undergrad majoring in business and an aspiring writer. Allpoetry.com/astrid_tejero

[ Jacob Mashburn ]

# Fall

I play in leaves under the tree
And my heart has now been set free
And left to bask out in the sun
And this is what I do for fun

Going fishing down at the lake
In the water the dog does shake
Eating my favorite ice cream cone
Suddenly my mind has been blown

Shopping at the store in the mall
Playing outside with the kids ball
This is my favorite time of year
It will come to an end I fear

The cold is coming by nights end
Now this is Summers only friend
I must now share the light of day
Now while all the children do play

---

I am originally from northwest GA. I have recently taken up writing poetry again as a hobby and it helps me with my thoughts and to clear my head. Allpoetry.com/Atmjo105

[ Vernoica Thibodeaux ]

# Sisters of the Blood Chalice

At night when you close your eyes, fall awake and meet me in the land of dreams. Where the Sisters of the Blood Chalice dance around sacred fires and call upon the Moon Goddess. We are in good company; the call of our sisters, Earth beating her drum (thump, thump...) and Sea running wild in the distance. Join our dance

---

I am from Lake Charles, Louisiana.I graduated the Delta School of Business and Technology. I enjoy music, art, nature and esoteric spirituality Allpoetry.com/Vernoica

[ Tanya Kanakaole ]

# Snug Harbor

Unloquacious cloak disguising our repudiate requiem.
Camouflaged alibi, what a ostensible motive.
Alchemy a stimulus for desire and consequence.
Eccentrically inclined to wrap myself up in your world.
Seeping into your skin, crawling through your mind
There's no detaching or letting go.
Take me to Snug Harbor, my love.

---

Writing poetry is a continuous enlightening experience. Most of my poetry is first draft but discretely edited as I write. Its only getting better . Allpoetry.com/Luvlylibravenus

[ Mark Andrew James Terry ]
# Too Frost To Know

Awaiting a path
with sure steps
to vivify, she lies
on a blackened matt
in a well-rehersed
savasana pose,
imagining
an unseen route
in the ceiling's
yellow craquelure.

A magenta aura
wanting yellow
mists about her,
crying out
to be followed;
way leading on to way,

but I,
in a malapropos mindset,
I was too frost
in my indifference
to know.

Words are powerful. They soothe. They wound. They incite. They create space where none exists and pull our core to the surface. I live and work in Orlando, Florida. Thank you for reading. Allpoetry.com/Mark_Andrew_J_Terry

[ Stefan Roudan ]

# naked clown

Deep inside the deepest pocket of an old clown outfit
lays the bottom of an ocean deep, so deep as infinite.
At the bottom of this ocean lays a city made of gold
hidden by the cloudy waters and protected by the cold.
Deep inside this sleepy city there's a box that hold the truth
about love about forgiveness about never ending youth.
Deep inside of all these secrets there's a beating of a heart
and it's rhythm is connecting all the future with the past
You were once happy
Remember to laugh
Pockets can't hold tears
Hands can discover gold
Cities can be hidden
No box can hold secrets
Love can't be explained
Forgiveness can be learned
Youth it's a state of mind
Heart is the will to go forward
Forward becomes backwards
But somewhere in the middle
There's now.

Im from romania but i have been living in london uk for about 20 years now. i am a multicultural sort of person and my writings comes from own life experiences at extremes points of my life Allpoetry.com/Stefan_Rou

[ Annabelle Molyneux ]

# And She Danced

She danced,
like it was
the last swing of a nervous pendulum.
She followed the beat of her heart
until she thought her pulse was gone.
She waited like an inmate on death row
for this life to end with one zap,
like an overdressed manic-depressive,
haunted by her ridiculous grandiosity.

She came to her eight senses,
that everything was tragically beautiful.
She realized, like a slave,
that she did not own her body,
her temple.
The Almighty One in Many
is the author of her life.
She must obey, like a chemical equation.

She was an expecting teenager
in a Prozac world.
She was waiting for that knight
on his blazing white horse
to save her soul.

She was bleeding cellularly
because she had gorged on rat poison.
Until her knight came
and rescued her.

Picasso and Van Gogh
were two of the eccentrics
that made her life interesting
with vibrant colors,
with elusive meaning.
She tried to paint like they did,
but all she saw was mud.

She contemplated, like a Buddhist monk,
what life had to bring.
She believed in the seeing Creator,
who knew her,
young and aged.
No.
She could not live in silent agony.
Her joy was to fiercely serve
the God she adored.

She danced
as if the world would stop.
She talked, like a hummingbird's flight,
so no one understood.
She lived in a grandiose reality,

and could she rescue herself
from falling into the pit?
She breathed cautiously; she knew
she still had a gambler's chance.

She whispered goodbye,
but she knew, under her nails
she still had gold to share,
to look at blushing nature,
to see the cold sky.

She was a nuclear woman
who would dance all night
with the hunter who found her
when she was lost--
her love, her better half,
her helper, her husband.

The tired pendulum kept swinging,
and she hoped it would not stop.
She loved it
because it would not quit.

She cried out, "Hallelujah!"
She was heard.
Her life was a reflecting pool.
The Spirit whispered in her ear,
"Be still. You are guided."

She stood up
and danced again.

---

Annabelle Molyneux was Writer of the Year in 2001. She majored in journalism and graduated with highest honors in 2005. Annabelle lives in Salt Lake City, Utah, with her husband, Max. Allpoetry.com/Bembie

[ David Michael Williams ]

# The Whispers of The Night

Still, somber, quiet, deep, and dark,
Something whispers into my heart.
A time, a place, at peace, I thrive,
Reminders that I yet remain alive.

Starlight upon an enchanted blue,
Wink down at me as they always do.
The trees rustle soft as if to say,
Tomorrow is hope in another day.

For now the world sleeps in its rest,
Listening to heartbeats within my chest.
Stay a while and let troubles fade from sight,
And listen to the whispers of the night.

---

Mike Williams is a poet from Texas. 'Poetry became my passion to express myself in literary form and cope with life's trials along my journey. The word well spoken and a deed well done is liberating.' Allpoetry.com/Mike_Williams_1

[ Stuart W. Bowen, Jr. ]

# Oh, Jesus!

I stopped my truck en route to you and Jesus
jumped right in. I thought "my God, you're Jesus!"
and He gently said "that's true my friend,
now would you please drive us on down this road."

I turned up sixth and took us through a pelting
rain that felt like pulsing pain pressing
on my broken town. "Stop here" he said
"let's get a beer and talk." we stepped into
a dim-lit pub and took our seats; I ordered
ale, He got the bock, and then we drank
a toast to all the fun that soon would fill
my frothy life. He prayed and broke some bread --
then disappeared!

"My Lord, my God!" I cried
and fell upon my knees surprised by joy!

---

Stuart is from Austin, Texas, married to Adriana, and dad to Nathalie, who is six. He plays guitar in a band, likes going to the gym, and is thankful for allpoetry.com. Allpoetry.com/SnookyB

[ Mary C Galindo ]

# Nature's Miracle

Did you hear that song?
The harvest fly's song
after his 17 year long nap
announcing the coming rain.

A miracle of nature .
as a sweet song was heard
and a midnight rain fell.
A witness to the miracle .

The rain very much welcomed.
The heat of this summer
seemed more intense than usual.
A balance of nature-another miracle.

Are there miracles giving us
a witness to the higher order?
For me there is no doubt.
the order of a creator.

---

Mary (grandmakay) is from N.D, lived in Guatemala, El Salvador, Venezuela. Currently living in Utah. She has always loved writing and poetry. Writing calms a reflective spirit. Allpoetry.com/grandmakay39

[ Christine Pingry ]

# Winter's Break

A feeling colder than ice, chills run down my spine.
White flakes of innocence fall to the frozen ground.
Somehow I know this years a turning point in my young life.
Looking out the frosted window wishing I was out there.
I have an old bag packed just in case I decide I'm brave enough, I've
learned to be prepared. You never know when you'll get the chance, if you do you better take it.
Run far and run fast, anywhere is better than here.

The air outside is colder than my heart, for now.
Resentment is building faster than my vocabulary.
This was the year I decided I'm a writer, five years old.
Hours of hiding, gives you hours of writing practice.
Determined my words will take me away from here.
I dream of leaving, it's my most comforting dream.

---

I was born and raised in New York. With a passion for writing since I was five years old, it's always been a part of me. Writing is my strongest form of expression. Allpoetry.com/yankee4590

[ Kali Krontz ]

# Eager

Twisted imagination
eager to get well
how many more pills will they subscribe this disorder
counteracting one another

I can feel the devil pulling at my character
fighting that urge to write myself off
should i take that plunge into the deep water
no life-jacket, no safety net to catch me

looking deep within the mirror bare skin
I see a body, as I smirk attempting to tell myself I'm good-looking
trapped by anxiety, paranoid I am unloved
I feel disliked by mostly every person

eager to stop taking medications to hush my troubles
tick tock ; looking at the clock hours melt into milestones
anxiety runs high as I pace the halls
pulling at my hair screaming inside
my voice is silent; I am not heard

Twisted imagination

eager to get well

how loud must I scream until I am heard

disorder is slowly taring me apart from inside

I am fragile and unsteady

Get me the fuck out of here

heal me damn it

I plead

As I stare out the barred windows...

---

The poet Killak is from Elmore, OH. Poetry has brightened her darkest days. She has been writing for 18 years. She is a young mother of one adorable two year old. Married to her best friend. Allpoetry.com/The_poet_KillaK

[ Claudia Sprague ]
# comfort food

teeth
were made
to strip away the surface
let the carnage ooze out

but I find
that while some see me as meat to chew
others take pride in preferring a peach to bruise

still my heart wasn't made to consume
with fruit they squeeze
until they find what they need
they suck it up to quench their thirst and call me sweet
then look for more tenderness to bleed

let's not pretend you aren't still a predator
when you wanted to drain me then leave me useless

---

Claudia Sprague is from a small town in Kansas. While she is currently working on getting her degree for psychology, she loves to write in her free time whenever she feels inspired. Allpoetry.com/Claudia_Sprague

[ D P Morgan ]

# I fell again today.

I fell again today, it gave me such a fright.
I was walking down the street and happened to turn right.
I tripped. I fell. I sprawled out upon the floor.
I stretched my length, from Daily News almost out the door.
My dignity ran out of luck as I hit the floor

To my aid rushed many, concern about each face,
Except the man that owned and ran this marketplace.
He was concerned, I am sure he was most sore,
For how can you sell a paper when someone's on the floor.
And someone with all aid, rises from the vinyl,
And reassuring rescuers, his fall was nothing final.
A bruise, a scratch from such a fall,
He's seen before and suffered all.

---

British Army Veteran with 13 service. Fan of Honda Goldwing. Recently retired and returned to writing. Writes poems about conflict, disability, politics and has short stories in the Steam Punk genre. Allpoetry.com/Dpmorgan

[ Susanne Donoghue ]

# Why?

Why do they fear black so
and force it to bleed red?

A crow's feathers are glorious spill
of glossy ink;
a horse's hide shines brightly in rain;
an African's skin glows blue-black,
like a swan's wing folding.

Forest nights with no reflection
are made for ears to swallow,
crickets, frogs and secret things
fill the dark with raucous song.

And yet police will kill the black
because they're scared, they say.
Perhaps it's just because they can,
easier than finding an excuse for jails.

I hate this fear, this crippling thong,
binding hearts to misery,
blinding us to hands that beg for life,
like any other hands.

Californian living in Ecuador, committed to creating learning communities to address acute ecosystem threats. Poetry for me is vision. Allpoetry.com/Susanne_Donoghue

[ Ketriana Yvonne ]

# Water is Life

Some came to sacred space.
Others were apart of the land
oneness with nature and man.

Trees sway much to say.
some obey others ignore.
Use force and yes even kill.
Natural flow of life is the
streams free flowing.
water for life.
Respect that death is palority
of life we are one with all.

Indian removal taught tribes
not to trust lessons learned
and not to be repeated.
Tribal treaty sovereign status
disrepected before.
No surprise remember
who were
killed the first time around.
Smallpoxs were the gift
they gave to steal
now same want to drill

now go

against treaty just

because

they are greedy.

The people are standing
like the tree for all to see.
Children are dancing now
Honoring the heritage of the
cultures power.
Ancestors were killed for
dancingto forget the
culture's power.

Rain dance must continue
Standing Rock
protect the ancestral grounds.
Pipelines must go
respect sacred soil
take yourself back
to where you came.
Dance on people
Water is life.

---

Ketriana Yvonne is from Brooklyn, New York.. She writes to inspire and awaken the sleeping as Spiritwriter. Ketriana is a Bricmedia Producer and entrepreneur causing change through poetry. Allpoetry.com/Spiritwriter

[ Holly Parker ]

# Live in the moment

Live in the moment

Not in the past

Embrace each day like it's the last

Mistakes will arise

As lessons are learned

Love will be made

And hearts will be hurt

Look to the good

Not to the bad

Recognize the chances to be had

As most can agree

It's best to say that wasn't for me

Contrary to I wish I were you

---

I am from Chillicothe, Ohio. I am a mother to 3 boys, work consumes almost all of my time. I am new to writing but I find it very relaxing. Allpoetry.com/Holly_Parker63

[ Nancy Mendi ]

# Southern Charm

Fiddly Dee look and see what I can see roses bloom and thorns bite
Fiddly Dee see what I see.
Fiddly Dee come play with me.
In the streams and through the fields and up the mountain top but, don't forget to skip rope so you don't lose hope.
Fiddly Dee won't you play with me.
Fiddly Dee won't you dance with me
The old folk are asleep
Time to be turning things red
Fiddly Dee dance with me?
Fiddly Dee I wanna watch a sunset instead.
Light the old pit and a roast some marshmallows.
FIDDLY DEE let's just cuddle instead.

---

Hello, my name is Nancy. I'm born and raised in NY. Thank for taking the time to read the work of a new writer. I only hope you enjoy it. Allpoetry.com/Phoenix_Raising

[ Tristan P. Scarbrough ]

# Yuki-Onna

Frozen over, warm-graced again;
That feeling of beauty;
fragile, fleeting.
Like the storm
that sees me fall upon this mountaintop.

Pale of skin, blackest hair;
it speaks to me; picks me up.
Such melodies of lilting sleet,
a bond eternal of no escape
that I'd care to wish or seek.

Such a muse speaks dreams of fantasy,
a stable life with family;
the brilliant rays of longing needs
forgotten to this bone white sea.

And as I speak, it fades away;
as I reveal, it deigns of me.
"My soul you take, in total succor.
My bonds you break in hunting snare."

Upon such words, I become myself again;
a standing figure to the bite of snow.

Tristan is from Arlington Texas. Poetry is the mechanism through which he writes observations on social experience, nature, and whatever particular pigment finds its way to the canvas of his reality. Allpoetry.com/Silverfish

[ Anamarija Celinić ]

# I still do

Cold expands through my chest
when brittle walls lean on me.
Something strange flees through
the voids between my ribs.
My eyes drift the empty room
avoiding the abandoned sheets
and the crammed rambling bags;
they lurk through slightly opened door.

Pretending you don't see me,
you put on your brown dirty shoes;
separating them from mine
just like mothers sometimes
pull their children's hands
when they want to pet a dog.
I thought your eye sockets
filled with sorrow speak to you.

My hands will not stop you;
they have always been weak
before your resolute glance.
I can't allow myself to speak out,
I don't want to leak in front of you.
But I put my muted heart in the pocket

of your rumpled jacket. So if you
ever wonder if I love you, it will sing:

"It is all right. I still do."

_____

From Croatia. I write because it makes me feel real. I love to listen and observe the world around me. Allpoetry.com/Passing_Observer

[ Deb Brat ]

# Thoughts can be blank

Thoughts are white
Thoughts are black
but if thoughts become blank .
Do you know when our thoughts become blank ??
When eyes are closed
and voices are choked
by a force from hell
thoughts become blank.
When conscience becomes slave
and habit becomes addiction
thoughts can be blank.
When souls become hollow
and minds are purchased
thoughts can be blank.
When hearts stop to beat
and the nerves become rusty
thoughts become blank.

———————

Debabrata Das loves to write Poetry since his school days. Despite being a management professional & college professor , he manages his time for his first love - poetry. Allpoetry.com/Deb_Brat

[ Charlie Rankin ]

# A Cosmos of Darkness and Light

There once was a boy who could dream a lost world
and manage to reach it at times;
his mind was a plaything that whispered and whirled
in realms he imagined and thoughts he unfurled
of heroes but also of crimes.

There once was a man who remembered it all
with much he would beg to forget:
The statements, the lies, the oft brazen gall
conceived of in pride but soon spreading a pall
on that which he came to regret.

There once was a corpse with no thoughts to embrace,
no dreams and no memories, no lies,
whatever the spirit now flown without trace
of heaven or hell for to dwell in the grace
which only from death could arise.

There once was a world set with promise sublime
which lived by the natural laws
but found itself bullied and badgered in time,
yet sung its most sacred and unending rhyme
in spite of its human born flaws.

There once was a cosmos of darkness and light
which sprang from the Great Nevermind
to be of itself with no wrong and no right,
no matter how boundless not fail to unite
all things and ideas intertwined.

---

A 69 year old retired registered nurse, and retired actor. I don't consider myself a true poet but rather more of a writer of verse, rhymed and/or metered or neither. Allpoetry.com/Charlie_Rankin

[ Emma Wilson ]

# Him

We are both vulnerable, with our cards on the table,
our stories spill out of our mouths as if they're words we
speak everyday and not dark secrets trapped in our
minds.
He sees the tangled wires in my brain and accepts that he
isn't an engineer and i don't expect him to be.
When our eyes meet,
everything disappears and it doesn't matter that my hair
is everywhere and my eyes are tired;
because I know he's not looking at that,
he's looking at me.
And i've never felt more beautiful.

---

A girl with a past, who writes poetry to distract her from her dark thoughts. She also collects unicorns.
Allpoetry.com/iwillsurvive

[ Paul Miller ]

# My first poem as an adult.

The waves are kissing the rocks

The boats go sailing by

Looking in the dark blue sea

Memories I have had

Days I lived

Never will I swim these waters with you

I begged you

Stay

Don't let yourself fade away

A great party I had

Family were there

Not you

The love of your life

The end of your life

A great man, a good man, a lovely man

Oh how I know

Just once more kiss my head

And say

Everything will be okay

Swim with me once more

Dad

My first poem as an adult - was not intended to be one. A wanna-be writer from Kilsyth, Scotland. I love reading and have always enjoyed novels. Books have been a passion for years but I have only discovered I like poetry within the last year. Allpoetry.com/Paulo9sm

[ Dakota Grinslade ]

# Hatchet

Sometimes... I lie to be alone
All ways I've tried and never died

To look upon your Starling eyes
it makes me disappear from your heart

Death wings spread and I am faint
I fear you've forgotten
My dear crucible; grace upon high

Silhouettes of demons are all I see
in naked trees of treasons at high noon light

Digging, is the feathered will
You're always bleeding on my good knives!

These walls and what they seem to be hiding,
haunt my way to you...
and your precious safety is nova

———————

27 years old. Type 1 diabetic. Born and raised in Panama City, FL. Open to interpretation; this poem is one in a series of short stories and prose poetry entitled; 'Thorned Tales and Other Maddening Haunts' Allpoetry.com/Dennis_Evahi

[ Nicholas Scott 'georgie' ]
# Silence Falls

Silence is all
that remains
no desire
to call your name

There's emptiness
gone the pain
Our history
hangs in a frame

Dancing dramas
lived and died
to leave a void
where I once cried

Silence falls
to end my dreaming
I close my eyes
and find no meaning

———————

I'm transgendered, male to female - I appear as male but my personality is female. Georgie is my female name. My interests include cosmology and science. I live in the UK. Born 1961 Allpoetry.com/Nicholas_Scott

[ Mikhail Dmitrievich Bashkirov ]

# The Better

If I could choose the doors into my life
In perfect sphere of crystal, through the time
Into the fragrant summer bloom I'd dive
But would you recognize my weathered lines?

While Morpheus would take you to his dome
There with the breeze I'd whisper nightly songs
And shadows of the August night would roam
The forest trails, the fields, the silent roads...

I know not, how and when we'd gone astray,
With years whizzing by like dragonflies
The starlight from the welkin was erased,
I saw fatigue and pain in mournful eyes

I held your hand so gently, but we have
Become the sculptures of antiquity
In stone forgotten, frozen, 'til the dawn
Restores our bedraggled broken dignity

No light is bright without lack thereof,
We learn to firmly stand by falling down
No night is night without early singing
Of birds awoken by the rays of Sun.

If I could choose the doors into my life
In perfect sphere of crystal, through the time
Into the fragrant summer bloom I'd dive
And tell you, in the end - all things are fine.

---

Pristine Silence is the pseudonym that best describes my inner self. It is the ultimate challenge of self-expression, to write of the ineffable. Allpoetry.com/Pristine_Silence

[ Stephen Hollins ]

# Turquoise Light of Aitutaki

John Williams left the island
back in 1821
and now they're all converted
Truly each and everyone

"Kia Orana" shouts the Reverend
Means "May you live a long life"
"Keep shining fellow Christians
it will keep you out of strive

Forget not to be grateful
for our turquoise translucent sea
this hook-shaped Aitutaki's
lagoon for the world to see

Forget not all our flowers
friendly people everywhere
smile to all our new whanau
say 'slow down folks - you are here'

Look at your Gothic windows
stained glass portals shine and glow
Let us sing to all in Heaven
a Traditional Hymn we know"

One hundred Aitutakians
Bursting loudly into song
overlapping harmonies
proving doubting Peter wrong

Immense power and unity
pure intention loving grace
shake my body soaring high
transformed by this gentle race

This mighty river swirling
whirling voices lift me up
bones and cells touched to my being
Children of God fill my cup

And yet they keep on singing
men women separate and same
all passion dedication
In the light of bliss I came

Tears pouring from my eyes
humble body I confess
my heart is reawakened
Aitutaki I am blessed

Yes my heart reawakened
Aitutaki I am blessed

"Kia Orana" shouts the Reverend

"Aitutaki we are blessed"

———————

I am loving writing poetry I live on Waiheke Island New Zealand. I specialise in Improv for Theatre and the work place, Story telling, Dance, Clown, Mime, Teaching, Building. Allpoetry.com/Stephen_Hollins

[ Patricia A Edwards ]

# Beyond the Desert

Beyond the desert the mountains touch the skies
From where we started long ago
To the day when God again took you away

We crossed many deserts barren and dry
We climbed many mountains not quite touching the sky
We slipped at times into the valleys low

We crossed the waters both deep and shallow
faced the days both dark and light
sometimes talking late into the night

I was sent to bring you home to him
In me you found the way out of sin
So Your new life would begin with him

So our final days we spent sharing love
The time we spent crossing that desert
Barren and dry to the land of love by his side

Now I must face the desert again
Until the day the sand goes away
and I again can see you with him.

May he guide me too as he did you
through the storms and the desert too
I so much want to be with you.

_____

Patricia is from Masury, Ohio. I use poetry as a way of expressing my inner self and coping with my feelings. I feel that I if i can help one person cope then I have achieved my goal. Allpoetry.com/Sweetlady53

[ Raymond Butt ]

## anemophilous Currents..

i don't always understand the rustic impediment of their
divers Speech
------ - She has her own volley, to Mean and royal Shape
shifter
i have my real to next image
- falling as i do
under her Spell
- - and unintelligible dynamo
lockheed with a Primordial degree
---- - unfolding in regretful omission
Atum's Offering Caused the burly Stars
- like unto goodly Pearls
My desire had androgynous and Concentric turning
rings
---- - - half buried in ataractic White light
- listening to the inaccessible and distant,-
---- Secluded analytical Voices
- My inconsolable father in impolitic recess
to drown my anthem
- ----- that which i long to hear
drawn from Pale blue lips

\- and receding onto the branch of my unobtrusive Stroke

----- anemophilous Currents

to the asymmetrical bridge

\- with insipid fascination?

So high they are ------

\- and dreadful

i will lacerate them to attenuate

-------  - - - reaching well past the linen Sinews

or in trickling fundamentality to govern and forewarn

\- it's quiet i know

the dictum is in her kiss

- - - - - - bellowing underwater

i thought it Could have been you?

\- Chattering incessantly about Miracles

glossy through the Womb?

-- - or in dramatic Point, lift and Sequestered arpeggio?

the Coruscating alternative was born detached from a glowering Sun

i was there -

\- there were three

admonishing themselves for being all too human

\- Sealed forever in a transposable and Constitute Monsoon

and forbidding illuminated procreation

i Cannot leave

---- - Sweep thou over an atmospheric Purloined Sea

or beat with indeterminate rapture

-- i find them entirely

Correlated through the deep

- here florid beside your towering Walls

i needed your judicious Covering

- - ----- as you recollect all of my doubtful Want

holding fast to our Covert,-

- and engaged Subterranean attachment

---- Stepping onto a lattice beam

i find them lying at the terminated Surface of your frigid breach

- that which is in Mottled flesh is never So Contained

--------- only lettered to Pause

- not for true devotion

--- - remarkably,

-- you should only transcend with your bruited feet

neither these black arts

dipping out of the Channelled depths

-------- exhale slowly thou you my raven

breathe acutely,-

---- immersed into your tampered lungs

- as She in neoteric Sands will tenuously Send them forth

rushing to love

Placated?

\-\-\-\-\-\- using rusticated entryways?

\- \- if no longer Constant?

roaming out of Moonglade,.. out of Moonglade

- reconsider from whence you came

Spinning into variegated rejuvenation..

\-\-\-\-\- they lost the egg.

---

Gabriel Walsh is from Ontario, Canada.. he has been writing poetry for over a decade. His interests include listening to U2 and pipe collecting. Allpoetry.com/Gabriel_Walsh

[ Jaira Zeck ]

## (like a rose)

i don't know why i thought maybe
we were real lovers
(you fucking fool)
(you thought it was going to last, too)

we climbed into the car
looking shy and inadequate in the back seat
yanking the paperness out of my heart
had nothing to do with the lack of
a rear view mirror, or absence of his shirt

a sniff under each arm
had him saying that i smelled
(like a rose)
he seemed somewhat sweet
until he started the engine,
gave a wave,
and drove off

i would have confronted him about
my blank pages and his lies,
but supposedly this was what we were wanting,
i just don't know why

the pressure of having to create something real this time
led us both to a disturbing restlessness of odd acts

several times,
i heard him say the night was over
during the day, even
he would remake a paper mâché heart
out of pieces of scratch paper made for me,
crumple it up,
and make it again "properly"

he would turn innocent (like a rose)
every nice day
as if the weather was in control
of who he was
he would snap out of it
when it wasn't the same nice day
just because he depends on the feeling
of each and every handmade sky
(like a rose)

it doesn't mean he's a pessimist
it just means he bit a man's head off
for giving me the wrong look,
and yelled at me for walking too far behind him,
leading me to have a brief fantasy
of what it would be like to live
(like a rose)

———————

your average angsty teenager on the path of becoming, somehow constantly loving who i am and the world around me. i never capitalize anything, but you didn't get mad at e.e. cummings, did you? •INTP• Allpoetry.com/starlet

[ Niky Smith ]
# No Light Without Darkness

the black of night brings out
the brilliant sparkle of stars long gone

the black of darkness allows
the suns almost unbearable bright

the black of hate lines silver
the scorching pleasure of love

the black of sorrow unveils
the lustrous spectrum to heal

---

I am no one. I am everyone. I am you and me and all of those who aren't seen. I want to write the words that speak to the soul...and convey the feels to young and old. Allpoetry.com/Ryanychole

[ Carolyn J Bayne ]

# Peace Maker

No more war,Knocking at our door,Create a little space,In this entire human race,End the plight of poverty,Such an atrocity!Peace and love to all,And having a lovely ball.This is our world to be told,For all of us to be bold,Working to earn a living,Let us start giving,To those less fortunate,For it will be either sink, swim or bus.It's just a tale of two cities,Within the communities,Stop attacking one another,Live life like a brother,Or sister,It doesn't really matter,We are all one like the other,Life is certainly too short,Less you decide to abort.Again, this is the world we are living in now,So at least, it's time to take a bow.

---

Carolyn J Bayne was born in Chalfont St Giles, Amersham and raised and educated in Oxford, England. She graduated from Ruskin College, where she studied, Creative Writing. Allpoetry.com/carolyn_bayne

[ Kathleen Hannah Marshall ]

# love is like a passionate night out

love is like a passionate night out,
where everyone is drinking a pint of ale,
no one knows the sorrow of where love comes from,
and it is a night of passionate sex and envious love,

passionate love is full of disturbing kinky sexual themes,
full of chains and whips and all things big and small,
but all the joys of luscious nights out with everybody,
all night of sex, drugs and alcohol with unbearable desires,
to have fun and make a deal with a cheating wife or husband,
leaving them to get on with there desires and things wild and free.

---

I think I have been truthful about what my poems are about and some of them are adults only some of them for kids and some of them for all. Allpoetry.com/Kathleen_Marshal

[ Geoffrey Barnes ]

# Her

He became acquainted and perceived that it was pure, the life inside him churned as he yearns for an abundance of HER.

The physical embodiment and personification of absolute perfection.
Between the radiating smile and the timid little grin,
Illuminating his soul wishing to make HER his own.

With doubt and lacking courage he remains under the shadow of persistent cowardice, continuing to build pressure in his proverbial bottle of emotions.
Alas, in some crazy reality where his ambiguous utterance has any degree of clarity; forever wishing the moment would arrive.

How can he promote his passion? Physical nor verbal communication promotes any progression. What is impeding on the raw untouched emotion? What ambient being is causing such a hindrance between him and HER.

With courage high and adrenaline pumping through his veins, simplistic inquisition comes from his mouth.

HER voice pierced his soul, melting his fragile heart, "I understand" he facetiously shrugs off.

After only a moment of assessment his heart descended in his chest, he understood the non-reciprocal spark. He knows there is a multitude of eligible men.

Why did he expect to stand out from the beastly competition? His lack of physical perfection continues to eat away the last of his confidence.

Can he settle for friendship? Or will the desire dissolve his sanity? He can't know what the future will hold, as he lays in an empty bed he contemplates the uncertainty of existence.

Through every day, every hour, every minute, every moment, every thought is riddled of HER.

All that is on his mind?
HER.

---

I started writing poetry after being inspired by the harsh rejection of a relationship, I found such a solice in it and couldn't stop. After all the positive reviews I couldn't help but continue. Allpoetry.com/Geoffrey_Barnes

[ Bosadiq Hashim ]

# The Spark

Derisive laughter shatters my hope
as sharp and piercing as a kaleidoscope
I clamp my ears tight but fail
to stop the torment that makes me frail

I close my eyes to the void of thought
to save me from this wretched drought
From the void I see the spark
effulgent, and blazing consuming the dark

All it takes is integrity
to break the knots of enmity
I will not confront them with my hands
the light in my spirit is what commands

I will not let them reap my soul
defiant I stand, as an angry troll
When they spew their venom, my eyes will convey
the intangible message that no words can say

The fuel of bravery caresses my heart
a shadow of glee as fast as a dart
Motionless they stand like a ragged doll
with words of wisdom, you can conquer all

I am a Kuwaiti citizen. I have a scholarship to study medicine in the UK. I am currently undertaking a Foundation course in Manchester. I am a massive Arsenal fan. Allpoetry.com/Word_Enzyme

[ Michael Orem ]

# Tear The Leash

Societies awaken.
Authorities frightened.

When clouds are shattered.
And darkness scattered.

When demons imposed.
And their lies exposed.

New thoughts will emerge.
religions tend to merge.

Then the bads are defined.
And the goods re-defined.
And the thoughts are refined.

Then our thoughts are denied.
What are we? ....... Blind.

When the game is the same.
We look for blame.

Then new gods are born.
Our societies are torn.

And we all loose again.
And the masters remain.

When the masters battle.
We have to be their cattle.

If our past is history.
Then future is mystery.
And our life is misery.

Religion was the leash.
Societies change the leash.
But still; on the leash !

If we don't want the leash.
Then we shall tear the leash.

---

Michael Orem is from Toronto, Canada. He was born on January 30/ 1982 His favorite quote: Every one likes to answer the questions but no one likes to question the answers. Allpoetry.com/Michael_Orem

[ Vernoica Thibodeaux ]

# A Tribute to Aphrodite

This handsome man with dark black eyes,

Knew a pain so deep inside.

That Aphrodite conjured me,

My body rising from the sea.

His fearsome loneliness could kill,

A wound that only love could heal.

I held his hand, and touched his heart,

And that is where our story starts.

A passionate kiss, a private joke,

I was born to bring you hope.

But then he touched me deep inside,

A place where only love abides.

Like the sunshine piercing through,

Aphrodite sent me you.

To bring me joy eternally,

You have my heart

And Blessed Be!

---

I am from Lake Charles, Louisiana.I graduated the Delta School of Business and Technology. I enjoy music, art, nature and esoteric spirituality Allpoetry.com/Vernoica

[ Joanne Zylstra ]

# What I See

What do I see?
What can I do?
The sun blistering my eyes
How do I shade them from you?

The sun must be up
The heat on my face
Waking to darkness
Is my fate everyday!

The night has fallen
How do I know
The birds stopped singing
The toads are a go!

Everyday is the same
In the eyes that do not see
Can't wait for a cure
To see the faces I once knew!

Written with love by Joanne Zylstra for my son Andrew who went blind in November 2011 in a Horrific Car Accident. Married since 1984. Resigned from work 2011 to be a caregiver to my son. My daughter graduated from police foundations and civil law. Allpoetry.com/Mommy_Bear

[ Joanne Zylstra ]

# This Night

The sound of thunder in my ears,
The sight of lightening sticking near,
I wonder what the Gods have to hold,
On this night that is so bold.

The darkness settles upon my eyes,
I wonder what this night has for my prize,
Is it winds that surround me and take me far,
Or is it rain that floats that floats like tar.

I am not scared as this storm unfolds,
But fearful of the stories still untold,
Bring me peace and stop this night,
I'm trying to sleep now Goodnight.

---

Married since 1984. Resigned from work 2011 to be a caregiver to my son who was in a horrific car accident and became totally blind. My daughter graduated police foundations and civil law. Allpoetry.com/Mommy_Bear

[ David H Hussey, Jr ]

# We're Not The Ones

We're not the ones
who scream and riot,
and loot, when they
can't have their way.

We're not the ones
who shout down others
for merely trying to have
their say.

We're not the ones
who introduce expletives
into what is supposedly,
a "children's'" poem.

We're not the ones
who terrorize families
of CEO's, while in their
own home.

We're not the ones
who threaten dire harm
to those who challenge
the campus "think."

We're not the ones
who go out of their way,
to see just how low that
society can sink.

We're not the ones
who overturn cars,
and smash windows,
when the our team WINS!

We're not the ones
who project onto others,
each and every of our
various sins.

We're not the ones
who fully stand guilty;
but, alas, here lies the
great shame:

When things finally come
un-done in our once-great
nation, we will be the ones
made to take the blame.

---

I am from Tampa, FL. I have a B.A. in Specal Education from the University of South Florida (Tampa). I am interested at history and politics. I am, alas, a conservative! Allpoetry.com/boydefender

[ Kiki Weber-Suarez ]

# Words

Have you ever really thought about the impact of a phrase
a single word said wrong can change the course of days
Words can mend a heart or even touch a soul
they can build a person up and help them reach a goal

But they can also tear them down and change point of view
you could be the culprit and you never even knew
you say it in the moment and the moment passed
but for the person hearing it, the effects they may well last

It may alter a future, it might destroy dream
if you look inside them, words arent what they seem
don't minimize your power make your words and actions true
not just the ones you're spoken but the ones you didn't too

Silence can speak volumes and expressions will betray
even words unspoken can affect a life today
So, think before you speak and be careful what you do
because after all is said and done
The one you may affect us you

---

My life has been a journey of euphoric highs and devastating lows. Writing is as natural to me is breathing, and just as necessary. I have two amazing boys... they are my muse and my motivation!! Allpoetry.com/Kiki_WeberSuarez

[ Peter Boadry ]

# Dear Mom (Today's your Birthday)

Today's your birthday
I miss you dearly
This is heartfelt emotion
And a son shows his devotion
You'd be ninety eight today
If you did stay
I know your in heaven above
And I will always love
You
Sad and blue
Today
Any day for you!

---

I've had Few poems published in Anthology's, Boss at Christmas, Mailbox Lady, Mailbox Lady 2, Dear Mom (May 1, 2004), King of Love, and A Heart Beats with One Love, and 1 short story Rescue 911: UFO
Allpoetry.com/Frpass

[ Debra Digioia ]

# A Moment Away

Why are you in heaven,
when I am down here?
It doesn't feel right,
I miss you.
I talk to your picture every night,
I love to see you smile at me.

Can you hear me?
I hear you.
I hear whispers sometimes,
when it is very quiet,
and I feel a gentle chill
on my forehead,
as I fall asleep.
I know it is you kissing me.

Do you see the spider webs
from where you are?
Do they glisten
with the morning dew,
like they did when you were here?

The squirrels have been asking for you,
and the branches of your favorite tree

wave at your window each morning.
They love you.
They told me.

You are still my best friend.
Please watch for me,
as you promised,
I'll be just a moment away.

---

Debbie, an artist and poet, loves to paint, sculpt, create mixed-media pieces and found object art. She uses her art and poetry as an outlet for her feelings, and as a way to connect with people. Allpoetry.com/Debbie_D

[ Brenda Joyce Mixon ]
# God Is Looking At You

He is watching every move you make,
And your actions, good or bad,
He knows your whole life story,
Which will one day come to pass.

Don't forget to ask the lord,
To forgive some of those moves,
For you walk a straight and narrow path,
Some steps with an attitude.

All you need is a little faith,
That of a mustard seed,
To know that God is in your corner,
To fulfill your every need.

Don't do things you know are not good,
And think that he is going to forget,
Because he is the one and only,
Who is due our total respect.

God is watching you, my friend,
So think before you act,
And those of you on the other side,
Need to get back on the track.

Born in Texarkana, Arkansas in 1956 to the late Alton and Birdie Mixon. I am the sixth child in a family of twelve. I graduated with honors from Arkansas Senior High school in 1975. Allpoetry.com/Brenda_Mixon

[ Roma Zerangue ]

# "Mom"

You - 81 years young; WOW! It is true.
Still, times I look to you; you answer when I know not what to do.
Your voice is gold; soothing, calm, never cold.
No matter how old you and I get, mom, I still look to you.
This job that no other can fill...
Your kindness, your grace, your calm,
only you.
The love you give out, through and through,
year after year,
can not be bought, but can be shared,
by only you.
I ask myself, now what? What to do?
So, what can I do? Learn to be me, within you.

---

My name is Roma; I write and create because I love the spoken and written word. Denotation, connotation, metaphors, vocabulary, I love it all. Reading and writing relax me; I forget problems. Allpoetry.com/Roma_Zerangue

[ Pasquale F. Lorina ]

# Go Away

They keep coming one after another
There is no end to their entrance
My ears feel the clamor of elephants

Go away I scream, yet no one hears
Leave me alone, but no one cares
I cry out in anguish, no one listens

Should I drink of this cup?
Should I accept the pain that I feel?
Why did this happen what did I do

I must ignore the constant shadows
I must bar open the egress and let them out
I must live my life and ignore the pain

---

I am a free verse poet, whom also enjoys oil painting and gardening. I reside in Brooklyn ,New York, with my wife and two young daughters. Poetry is a catharses for me, It cleanses the soul. Allpoetry.com/Pasquale_Lorina

[ Dakota Grinslade ]

# Mayhem & Chaos

'In a world without dreams, we are doomed'
-Anonymous

Cody's the name
Chaos is to blame
for all of my actions lately

Matty's aflame
Soot for decades
in the wake of his ashes, waving

The spirit and joy of togetherness
The laughter, the tears
Echoes of the spirit of night
That is the sweetest music

Keep your closed eyes sleeping, seeing
Turning key words,
opening doors to new worlds

Up, up, up the stairsfrom regal dwellings beneath,
a child's impossible thoughts
stir in slumber

As long as you believe,
there will always be
a haven for your wonder
Childlike at heart
wishing upon stars;
don't lose that spark

Don't go fooling yourself
This is nothing
More than anything,

I wish, gazing into possibilities
that our dreams
are the first step to reality

---

Matty Mayhem & Cody Chaos. One of many nicknames my twin brother and I have for each other. Love you Mattio. This one's for all you dreamers. Follow your heart, love life and live it to the fullest. Allpoetry.com/Dennis_Evahi

[ Joseph Benjamin Hobbs ]

# € |-| o o $ 3 /\/

My People, problems, I solve them.
there is Never a problem;
  only situations and solutions.

So here I go:
Here I go;
  Showing, You, "WHO?" : I REALLY AM!!!

Uncle Sam can't save your @$$;
snakes in the grass;
  Going, a, round.
    Problem solvers solving puzzles painting perfect
pictures

My brothers and sisters, I know you.
I feel the pain, I have heard;
  Now I Am the Sheppard.

Everyday, I cry in my bottles
filling up real quick
  I Am the One I AM the Sun

So, Yo, You can have your fun;
poke and pick me up
I don't run anymore

this store is, "open" All Day
My oh my why?
All the gates of hell & hate?
   Dismayed ampersand pained
only creates Everyday!

I do not demand
I run commands
I process patches
I mix up big batches of good things
I do not lie nor do I deceive you;
I, Listen, I Please the hearts of men;

I wear my my hearts on my sleeves
So, so do you, not you, know what's on my plate.
Everyday I wake;
Knowing what's inside the store of overload memory hate.
I love the People, On watch Everyday.

---

I am just Joseph, just like you are you. I just know who I Am. I know Christ. Once you are enlighted there is no going back. In the past they died after enlightenment because of non acceptance. Allpoetry.com/Pinconesap

[ Annie Foster ]

# The Wilting Flower

Petal by petal,
You pulled me apart.
Till there was nothing left,
You broke my heart.

Where is the solid ground,
That you pulled me from.
I'm a broken mess,
And I feel so numb.

Every piece of me,
Is on the ground.
Always staring at me,
But make no sound.

One petal you wanted me,
Another petal we couldn't be.
One petal you wanted me,
Another petal too soon you see.

One petal you wanted me,
Another one gone from me.
One petal you wanted me,
Now you're confusing me.

Another day gone,
I'm wilting away now.
Another day gone,
I'll be okay somehow.

You plucked and plucked,
Till there was nothing more.
I would've loved you forever,
Deep down to your core.

You felt like home to me,
We could've figured out the rest.
You never really loved me,
I was only second best.

The person that you're with,
Should bring out the best in you.
They should make you love life,
And love all that you do.

---

Annie Foster is from Greeley, Colorado. She is 26 years old and is an avid writer. Writing helps her to cope with the things in her life that she can't control.
Allpoetry.com/Afoster

[ Ashley Cantrelle ]

# Your Love of Life or Life of Love? The Latter.

I hate love.

People say, "If the shoe fits wear it!"

What if their stolen shoes

that are caked with mud and dog shit.

Should I wear it then?

No thanks, I'll go barefoot.

You, however, love love.

You're young and new to societal lifestyle.

You meet a nice girl,

someone you could really love for the rest of your life.

But you mess things up on purpose

because settling down at your age scares you.

Some years pass,

everyone around you seems to be getting married.

You decide to get with the program.

You propose the girl you've been dating

because you're in love,

at least, that's what everyone tells you.

Things are good for a while.

You have a solid job and a mortgage,

you're also expecting your first child.

You argue with your wife over the simple things:

groceries, pets, baby shower dates,

friends, what to watch on TV, eating habits,

pornography, who does laundry, possible vacation,

what to wear, who cooks, house chores,

daily hygiene, etc.

But these are simple-sweet arguments,

almost always ending with sex.

Yes, you ride the waves of love's illusion.

Until more years pass,

and you totally wipe out.

You aren't quite sure

if your children ruined your marriage

or if it was already doomed to begin with.

But are sure of one thing:

you're horny.

Hump-the-small-space-in-between-the-running-washer-and-dryer kind of horny.

But your wife stopped putting out.

You think she's cheating on you,

but you don't want to bring it up

because you want to find someone else to fuck too.

And you do.

Then it blows up in your face when your wife finds out,

turns out, she was never cheating on you.

She was just tired.

You two love birds argue about divorce for months,

until you both decide to stay

on the pieces of a broken marriage

"for the kids' sake."

Many years pass,

you're old and fat

but still with the one n' only.

You gave up on true love a long time ago.

You don't love your spouse,

you don't believe you ever did.

But you can't imagine living with anyone else.

You bicker and bite at each other,

but it's nothing like what you used to do.

You wanted love, and you got it.

No one ever notices

that every love has an expiration date.

---

Ashley is from Baton Rouge, LA. She writes to seek out the truth of human nature, sink her teeth in the grey matter of it all. Allpoetry.com/CypressSideShow

[ Diana Viguri ]

# You Know My Name.. Grief

My name is GRIEF let me introduce myself
I'm here to wreck havoc on your life & wreck your health

I shall make you feel pain like nothing or no one else
I am the black cloud above the trees
I am the gut wrenching SADNESS that brings you to your knees
Come
Clouding your vision until you can't see
If you have ever had a worst fear here I am it's ME
I start off slowly than rise with debilitating intensity
You won't know what hit you asking whats come over ME?

There's a storm coming & its swirling just like the sea
I dont care wheather or not you agree or disagree
I am your new harsh reality

I have got no time for useless pleasantries
Better recognize I hold the lock and the precious key

Im in charge the Sergeant of this infantry
You will be obedient and bow down to me

Your Emptiness will go on for eternity
The circumstance boo hoo such a pity
I'm EVERYWHERE in every town & every City

I'm here to beat u up make you feel nasty and unptetty
I will drive some to drink others to use

What do I care Ive got nothing to lose
I will steal your energy and rob your smile
I will cause u self doubt keep u in denial

No one is safe the day will come when we all OWE
Once I latch onto u
I won't let go

You will try while I taunt you saying "I told ya so"
Im in your every thought every minute of every dayl
Until I'm back again ready to play

But this game is not the one of your choosing
This game your most defiantly will be losing
I don't show compassion or respect
The task is simple it's here to collect

Don't u worry It came for me it will come for you
There's only one thing to do
& this is key
But Don't say you heard it from ME
Deal with the grief head on and set it free

If not prepare to live your life in agony

And expect many more visits.. from yours truly

———————

Mrslilboo is a Jersey girl at heart but currently lives in CA. Been writing Poetry since age 12 to express feelings, wasn't until death if Beloved Mom iin 2016 she shared to help cope with loss. Allpoetry.com/Mrslilboo

[ Kayla Brothers ]

# Dreams

I put my mind to a different place,
hoping to get out of reality.
Chasing my thoughts,
wishing it would take me from this brutality.
I close my eyes
and dream of the galaxy.
A galaxy, where I'm free
From all worry and struggle.
A place I can obliterate and bury the troubles.
My thoughts are wary,
But my soul pursues.
If I had to choose;
between my dreams and reality.
I'd choose my dreams to take me from this tragedy.

---

Kayla Brothers is from Ola, Arkansas. I'm fifteen years old. I like writing poetry to express my feelings and maybe to help someone else going through the same troubles as I. Allpoetry.com/Kayla_Brothers

[ Rebecca Lyle ]

# Night

When I lay my head down to sleep,
I can feel your loneliness calling me;
can you feel my pain calling to you?
The emotional mess of what I've become,
seemingly unaware drifting alone
in your own world of perfect palisades.

In my dreams,
I am haunted by a creeping mist,
trying to find traces;
you are out there -
I can not seem to be able to find where;
helplessly skirting the unbearable
that will leave me with the just hurting.

You have to be aware of what you mean to me,
I have been completely
open to you always....
You are hidden in a murky cloud
out of reach --
just circling on the edges of your mind.

Leaving me writhing in kind,
hopelessly wondering, withering vine.

Will you ever let me in
or it is an eternity of uncontainable pain?
Is it my cross to bear,
the years will not be kind, my heinous crime.

Your inattentive attitude
always keeps me lost;
I am a kite lost in the wind,
blowing always further and further away,
as the child aimlessly runs,
calling, please, please come back to me.

It is draining me of what I am,
leaving only an empty shell of myself.
We have become the proverbial clique
that pounds in my head;
in the sea of life,
we are the two ships that pass in the night.

---

I am a poet and a writer and have been married for twenty-eight years, with 3 children and 7 grandchildren. I live in Cincinnati, Ohio where I went to the University of Cincinnati. Allpoetry.com/Rebecca_Lyle

[ Antonio Rivera Iii ]

# Yauco

She begins her day,
to the sounds of coqui singing, ripe mangos dropping
from tall trees.
She walks, down mountains, over fertile soil.
The tropic sun warms her skin, then bakes it brown,
tough
until she is indistinguishable from the dirt.
How beautiful she thinks,
an island that makes you look as alive as
the tilled and turned land you grow food from.
What a woman, to not only create a family from nothing
but unfair wages, calloused handed
and the dreams she will leave to her next of kin,
but to also create generations of her brown babies that
will thank her for overcoming every terrible man, boss
and bill that tried to stop her.

The sun honors this woman
Lights her path every morning
She goes to a panderia.
Because well, Puerto Rican's love their pasteles.
As she arrives they tell her – "Sorry, closed."
Closed she asks?

Forever the owner says.
Forever closed.

She continues into the town,
as she begins to grow tired.
Traveling from store to store
it is as if her town has all left her.
Closed, they say, forever
The land is sick, her land is sick
And she is her land, and she is sick
And the hospital, months away from closing
Diagnoses A, Diagnoses B, Diagnoses C,
Treatment Z, Treatment Y Treatment X
Ray scans left unread, and no doctors left to decipher
A fast-fading body
What an impossible task to heal heart and home
Treatment is possible, they tell her in a bigger city, elsewhere
And isn't it always better elsewhere, always
She is told she cannot be transferred by ambulance,
Empty caravans now promising no salvation
Trapped, she fights in an empty hospital room
Recalling some forgotten story about a prophet
Wrestling an angel – and didn't he lose?
And all she has now is her son's prayers

She begins her day.

To the sounds of dated heart beat monitors and bodies dropping from this world full of fears.
She lays, down on unkept bed and over soiled linens.
The nurses neglect her skin, until she is undistinguishable from trauma victims as bed sores ravage her body.
How terrifying she thinks, an island that makes you look as dead as concrete graveyards of forever closed dreams.
And the doctors say the labyrinth of misdiagnosis has made her resistant to every drug
And she wishes she could laugh at the fact that at least some part of her body remembered strength, and what a cruel kind to recall

Abuela, I say to my father, will make it because for a second I believe hope just might be enough.
But like acid rain during a drought, infected blood is nothing but a death sentence in the guise of a necessity.
I am sorry I tell my father, I was wrong.
I am sorry I want to tell my abuela, I didn't know what else I could have done.
I fear I will have to continue to apologize for my helplessness.
For every hospital closed and every doctor lost there are thousands of US citizens whom must share my families fate.
I cannot find any solace in mourning as this becomes

common, galleries of our dead
I have already buried my abuela.
I do not want to bury my island too.
She left me, with much bigger dreams than that.

---

Antonio Rivera is a college student from Austin, Texas. He attends school at Texas State University in San Marcos, Texas and is a sophomore pursing a Political Science degree. Allpoetry.com/Batmanmcginnis

[ Jason Robert Van Pelt ]

# Heart Omnibus!

Good day! Say there is Heart For All! Always remember, it plays like a trumpet

Love comes from its' writ, at the bottom up to the top summit,

Feelings felt are life dealings dealt, in a way some meals melt

Ceilings above while kneeling below, lo, know Madison poetry of Van Pelt,

Poeticism, 'tis the heart of art! Poems within helms & homes are very fine like combs

The United States of America shall remain impart of Earths' poetic realms & domes,

From in here and there on out, hearts shall be unbroken

Up for grabs in the open or on the mend, then spend a free token

To tend to the good word of love, of which is at its' best when spoken,

Mileage, pursue thy dreams as well as follow your heart anew

Baggage, ever get thy heart set on something that thou never knew?

―――――――――

Jason Robert Van Pelt was born in Madison, WI on August, 4th 1987. Poetry is Americas' culture. Poetry is Americas' foundation. Long live poetry! Poetry is for all! Allpoetry.com/Jason_Van_Pelt

[ Joanne Zylstra ]

# The Visit

I walk through the doors always locked to be safe,
The noises I hear are very well known for this fate.

I make my way over to the elevator to go up
Smiling and greeting; you know, the usual stuff.

I press the button and up I now go,
I head to the top, to the top I must go

In a flash the door is open, but it feels like forever,
I step on out and it feels much better.

The smells and the voices are always the same,
I head down the hallway, as if it were a game.

With love in their eyes and voices strained,
They try to remember, remember my name.

I love these two loving souls,
They make me feel warm no matter where I go,
I love these two loving souls,
Take care of them wherever they go.

I sit for a while, asking them questions,
Ask them how they are, not a bad word they mention.

It is now time to go, I retrace my steps,
But my heart is always a weeping,
I am truly a mess.

Take care my dear parents, I love you to death, and I will be back tomorrow after you rest.

---

Married since 1984. Resigned from work 2011 to be a caregiver to my son who was in a horrific car accident and became totally blind. My daughter graduated police foundations and civil law. Allpoetry.com/Mommy_Bear

[ Stefan Roudan ]

# Lets run

Let's run together from this place of madness
The time has come for us to get away
Lets leave behind the fear and the sadness
Let's run along the night until it's day.

Forget of him, he doesn't love you better
Flowers are meaningless once they are killed.
And tears are just salty weather
and trophies are but wishes unfulfilled

It's all a lie, you can't deny your feelings
All it's design to fuck up with your mind!
There are no other new beginnings
Unless you run and you won't look behind!

I know you know, freedom is the most precious
Yet you don't know what freedom is
Is just a word full of emotion
or is it just a place to live?

Come take my hand we're all above the oceans
nothing can stop us now, we are already gone,
The flight induced by senses is in motion
We cannot stop until the run is done

Im from romania but i have been living in london uk for about 20 years now. i am a multicultural sort of person and my writings comes from own life experiences at extremes points of my life Allpoetry.com/Stefan_Rou

[ Vernoica Thibodeaux ]

# The Tears of my Ancestors

My soul groans within me
with words that cannot be uttered.
The tears of my ancestors are my own,
they have taken root in the Earth
and sprouted in my Soul.
Tall as the cedars of Lebanon and
strong as the mighty oak

The tiredness of the bones,
the child snatched from its mother's arms,
the withered hopes, and dreams....
Beautiful flowers plucked before their time.

Blood running through the earth like water;
Africa crying for her children.
The back breaking beneath the weight of
too much pressure.

The un-song heroes and heroes
whose stories will never be told.
My soul is afire with your might.

So when I am alone in the presence of Spirit,
and I close my eyes to pray.
I have no need of words,
my Spirit groans
with the tears of my Ancestors

---

I am from Lake Charles, Louisiana. I graduated the Delta School of Business and Technology. I enjoy music, art, nature and esoteric spirituality Allpoetry.com/Vernoica

[ Geovanny Medina Arteaga ]

# A Forever Impure Life

I was happy once, happy as can be
How could I ever forget that day?
When, I lost everything...
Almost midnight, intoxicated...
Partying, having fun for the very first time..
How I mindlessly met you...
I was an angel, you were the serpent
I never quite saw such grace and beauty in my lifetime...
You were so irresistible and tempting..
Those looks and dark affections you expressed to me..
How could I resist?
I touched your smooth soothing skin, you groped me in such a wicked lovable way
In those few moments I could of sworn I heard my parents voices repeating to me, "Don't do it! Resist! Come back to us! Don't be tempted!"
I madly laughed and slowly...I looked into your eyes
I saw evil, and evil saw me
I felt my purity being sucked and stolen from me
You laughed at me and said, "You should of listened to your parents."
And at that moment I knew...
I had eaten the apple

I had disobeyed

Therefore, I must pay the ultimate price...

The price of a forever impure life

---

Geovanny Medina Arteaga is a teenager living in Las Vegas, Nevada. Experiencing the world day by day. Pursuing a career in a public library, and is known for writing meaningful love related agonies. Allpoetry.com/Geovanny_M.

[ Arthur C. Liggins ]

# Just Like You

Just Like You
Every parents dream is to have a child grow up and be very special
Just Like you
But Like dreams and wishes, all things don't come true
Not Like you
Every child is unique in their parent's eyes, and then there are those that are special and take living to a brand new hi
Just like you
To say I am proud is just one phrase I could mention, I knew you were special, for as a baby, you would scream (not cry) if you weren't getting attention, but it turns out to be
Just like you
You have reached heights that most black men and women will never reach. I love it. It shows a reflection of Me.
Just like you
But forever stay humble because first you are a child of God.
And forever my little girl, for just like you – you are you.

Arthur C. Liggins lives in Memphis, TN and his battling cancer. His daughter is submitting his poem that he wrote for her on her birthday 11 years ago.
Allpoetry.com/Kliggins1908

[ Ronald Watson-Bolden ]
## Black Like Me

If you were black like me

Through my eyes the world you would see

Life is not always what it may seem

If only this hell was not real but a dream

If you were black like me

You would not ask a lot from life

Just to be free from bigotry , prejudice and strife

If you were black like me

You would understand what it means to truly not be free

---

Ronald Watson-Bolden Jd Med. Poetry is a outward expression of my life as a black man in a white world . My writing gives me a way to express my view of the world through my eyes. Allpoetry.com/Watson_16252

[ Stephen Kelly ]

# My Stand for Love

The stand I make for life and love,
These things I will be speaking of.

I come from a place where chaos rules,
Where love and affection are not the tools.

Sadness, grief, anger and reproach,
These were my mentors, my teachers, my coach.

They taught me to lie, to hide and fake,
My life, my loves, my feelings forsake.

All things good and decent and true,
Seem to come from far and few.

My time has come to begin a life,
No longer consumed by indignity and strife.

But to start to feel the feelings of love,
These are the things I now speak of.

Warmth, compassion, empathy and grace,
To act and do and find the place,

Where I can learn to show I care,
For every person, everywhere.

I once believed these things exist,
In a place that's far beyond my grip.

Yet here and now I finally see,
The place of dreams is also for me.

For it's not a place to travel to,
Or a destination for me or you.

It's in your spirit, your heart your soul,
This place is a thought that makes you whole.

I begin to see my truer self,
Distractions and arrogance fall from the shelf.

I start to feel this thing is real,
This thing called love which makes me feel.

Beauty, love and grace are here,
I embrace these things and toss my fear.

I now will love the things I greet,
And show that love to all I meet.

I will take love and give love in equal share,
No longer offering heartache or despair.

I offer up my life and my love,

These are the things I now speak of.

———————

S.G. Kelly lives in the Canadian Rockies with his wife, Barbara. They have two grown children, and live a quiet life nestled in a small valley. Allpoetry.com/SG_Kelly

[ Robert Moody ]

# They don't want you loving me

They don't want you to love me girl, and I know its true;
Started trying to separate us the first day I met you.
Try hard as they may to be kind and cordial toward me, but their facade is so obvious, even a fool could see.
They lock you away in a little hamlet, though regal in appearance it may be, this defying act they do, to keep you away from me. Although rare are the moments when they all have gone, I make haste to get to you, can't stand to see my baby alone. When I get there, my heart grieves for what it sees.
You sit there all alone in your lonely room, it's a little sad and filled with gloom.
I walk inside and I see your hiding place, I give you flowers, a gentle kiss, then a smile comes on your face.
They don't want you to love me, and it's plain to see, they say kind words but in their hearts they're throwing rocks at me.
Who is it they want you to love, it isn't me and I don't mind, just don't be smiling at me while hating me inside.

They don't want you to love me but that's ok, just stop telling me lies, take off the mask and show your face.
I call you on the phone, but they won't give it to you, they even tell me lies just not to put you through.
I feel so burnt- up inside sometimes, don't know what to do, wanna get back at 'em girl, but don't wanna wind up hurting you.
They don't want you to love me, and it's plain to see. They say kind words but in their hearts they're throwing rocks at me.
Who is it they want you to love, it isn't me, and I don't mind, just don't be smiling at me while hating me inside.
They don't want you to love me, but that's ok, just stop telling lies, take off the mask and show your face.
Just leave us alone, stop trying to control our fate, no need to fake kindness, while all the time concealing hate.
They can't conceive girl that it's me who you love, I bet you, living in darkness, blinded by ignorance obsessed with manipulation, they only upset ya.
Sho nuff girl, gonna tell'em where they can go; gonna tell, em what they can do; stay out of our lives; we don't wanna hear no more from you. Stop smiling at me, I know who you are, stop lying to me; you done it many times before, stop playing with me, I'm not your little

toy. Please leave us alone; we don't need ya.Stop playing your little games, you can no longer deceive us.
(Talk) Oh no, they don't want you loving me, don't won't you giving me love. Can't bear the thought of us being together. Can't see the fact our love is forever. That's too bad, too bad, yeah; it's so sad, so sad. Wanna stop us, yeah, they can't take it; tried every trick in the book, but can't make it
Come on girl let's go, gotta get out of this place, had enough of their shit; ain't got no more time to waste. Let'em keep on dreamin, that's what they're doing; let'em keep on scheming, desperately trying to undo us.. Adieu, good bye, adieu, so long; Adieu good bye; just gotta keep on moving yeah un hanh, just gotta keep on grov'in, yeah un hanh.

---

I live in the San Francisco Bay Area. I work as a counselor at The Santa Clara County of Behavioral Health. I like to write and play jazz keyboard.. I am an avid practitioner of Zen and Karate Allpoetry.com/Rmoody03

Made in the USA
Middletown, DE
22 March 2017